Sail & Rail

A Narrative History of Transportation in Western Michigan

By Lawrence &
Lucille Wakefield

For Philip
and James

Reprinted by Thunder Bay Press
Printed by Eerdmans Printing Company,
        Grand Rapids, Michigan

Library of Congress Catalog Card Number: 80-53570
ISBN: 1-882376-31-5

96 97 98 99   2 3 4 5 6 7 8

Holt, Michigan

Prologue

During the years when I was growing up in Chicago, which was then a rather pleasant place to live, my brother and I spent several memorable summers at a boys' camp in northern Wisconsin; and one of my most poignant memories is of riding the night train to camp from Chicago to Boulder Junction, Wisconsin, on the Chicago Milwaukee & St. Paul Railroad.

There were about twenty of us each year who gathered at the old LaSalle Street station in downtown Chicago — twenty boys of ages from ten to fifteen, all thrilled at the prospect of the long train ride. As I remember, the train pulled out around eight o'clock, and another twenty or thirty boys would come on board an hour later at Milwaukee. All of us had Pullman berths, and most would go to bed (if not to sleep) by ten or eleven. But some of the more romantic and adventurous of us would stay up all night long.

The train stopped at innumerable places between Milwaukee and our destination, and I remember what fun we thought it was to get off at each of the dimly-lighted little stations for the few minutes that it took to discharge the mail and the milk and to take on whatever was going north. Who wanted to sleep when the opportunity offered to experience so many strange new places in a single night? Well, some of the more sensible boys did, but my brother and I weren't among them.

I date my love of railroad trains from those night rides from the city into the heart of what was then an almost unspoiled wilderness. The mysterious little depots and the mysterious towns around them, the houses all dark and everyone in them fast asleep; the huffing of the steam engine in its impatience to get going again; the haunting sound of the signal bells at lonely street crossings — those memories will stay with me forever.

Like a great many other people I have a special affinity for railroads. I wish that I had been born in time, too, to ride the fabulous Great Lakes steamers. With the passing of the ships and the railroads, a way of life is gone forever. I doubt very much that anyone now has a feeling of nostalgia for the Model-T Ford or that anyone in the future will yearn to ride again in a Boeing 707 or even a DC-3. Automobiles and airplanes are fine, but somehow they just don't seem to generate the same mystique.

So this book is dedicated to all those people who are in love with the memory of ships and railroads: to the ones who rode them and, with sympathy, to those who never did.

Acknowledgements

This book could hardly have been accomplished without the help of a great many generous people whose kindness we can scarcely repay but can at least gratefully acknowledge: To Michael.McGuire and his staff at the Traverse City Public Library; Bernard Rink and staff at the Mark Osterlin Library at Northwestern Michigan College; once again to Lucille Zoulek, whose indexing of a hundred years of Traverse City newspapers on microfilm at the college library has been an almost indispensable tool in our research; to James Brinkman and George Gregory of Traverse City, and Robert Warrick of the Ann Arbor Railroad Historical Society, who read parts of the manuscript and made valuable suggestions and corrections; to Susan Gerhart of the Benzonia Public Library, Celene Idema of the Grand Rapids Public Library, and William Miles of the Clarke Historical Library at Central Michigan University. Special thanks also to Jennie Arnold of Traverse City.

We are also grateful to the many persons and institutions who were so kind in trusting us with the loan of valuable pictures and other graphic material: Edward Bardy, James Brinkman, Elden Dame, Guyles Dame, Cole Gronseth, Arlie Killman, Natalie (Noble) Kohler, George Littell and the Leelanau County Historical Society, David Johnson and the Manitowoc Maritime Museum, Frederick Honhart and the Michigan State University Historical Archives, Fred Parkinson and the Sleeping Bear Dunes National Lakeshore, Dave and Diane Taghon and the Empire Township Heritage Group, Fred Ritter, John Russell, Traverse City *Record-Eagle*, Robert White and Robert Winnie and, especially, Lynn James and the Pioneer Study Center.

And last but not least we are grateful for the continued patronage of James E. Dutmers and Empire National Bank.

Table of Contents

LaSalle's *Griffon*, first sailing vessel on the
upper Great Lakes.

Sailboats & Steamers

"And this also," said Marlow suddenly, "has been one of the dark places on the earth."

JOSEPH CONRAD
Heart of Darkness

From the Earliest Times

By Paddle and Sail

No one knows exactly when that marvelous invention, the birch bark canoe first made its appearance, but it must have been in general use among the eastern woodland Indians hundreds of years before the white men got here. It evolved from the floating log and the dugout canoe, which certainly were the earliest forms of water transportation in the Grand Traverse region. Later, in the middle 1600s, the great voyageur canoes of the early French explorers, trappers and traders — commonly thirty to forty feet long — must have coasted these waters. (There is good evidence of an early 18th century French settlement on Beaver Island.)

The first sailing ship on Lake Michigan was LaSalle's *Griffon,* built near Niagara Falls in 1678-1679. She was a wooden vessel about 60 feet long and of 45 tons burden. On her maiden voyage in the fall of 1679 she sailed across Lake Erie, up the Detroit River and across Lake St. Clair and Lake Huron. Having entered Lake Michigan on September 2 at the Straits of Mackinac, she dropped anchor a few days later somewhere near the mouth of Green Bay, possibly at Washington Island. (Most authorities say Washington Island, but George I. Quimby, curator of North American Archeology and Ethnology at the Chicago Natural History, makes a good case for Summer Island.)

LaSalle loaded the *Griffon* with furs from the area and waved goodbye as she departed on her return trip, while he remained behind. She sailed from Green Bay on September 18, 1679 — into oblivion. Nothing was ever seen of her again. Although several localities along the northern shores of Lake Michigan and Lake Huron (including Manitoulin Island) now claim to be her gravesite, no indisputable evidence of where she went down has ever been found. (Quimby suggests she was wrecked, in the storm of September 19 to 24, somewhere along the coastal waters of Michigan's Upper Peninsula between Point Detour and Epoufette — or possibly in the Beaver Island archipelago.)

The Mackinaw Boat

When Indian Agent Henry Schoolcraft came down from the Soo to Grand Traverse Bay in 1837, looking for a suitable site to establish an Indian mission (he checked out the Peninsula and also Marion Island, then called Island No. 10), he travelled by Mackinaw boat. And two years later, it was by Mackinaw boat that the two Presbyterian missionaries, Peter Dougherty and John Fleming, arrived at the little cove on the east side of Old Mission peninsula to found the first Indian mission in this region. Catholic missionary Frederic Baraga is also said to have visited the region by Mackinaw boat.

Thus the Mackinaw boat played a significant role in the early development of the Grand Traverse region. This particular type of small sailing craft was originally developed by the French, probably on Lake Huron, in the late 1700s. Although many small sailboats of various design were in the early days called Mackinaw boats, the type had become fairly standardized by 1840.

The true Mackinaw was a clinker-built, gaff-rigged boat, more or less of ketch design, though the two masts were about the same height. She carried a single jib, strung out on a long bowsprit. The boats varied in length from 14 to 40 feet, but the most popular was a 26-footer with a seven and a half foot beam. It was a graceful double-ended craft with a sharp bow and full cheeks, narrowing aft to a sharp stern. Because of its rather flat bottom and shallow draft — and its centerboard — the Mackinaw was an ideal work boat at a time when harbors and docks on the lakes were few and it was important that a boat could be easily beached. Indeed,

the Mackinaw's two masts were often used to roll the boat up on a sloping beach.

The Mackinaw was remarkably seaworthy. It sailed free, and despite its open hull could ride out any ordinary storm if someone was free to bail. The boat was commonly used for passengers and freight. Later, after the turn of the century, Mackinaw boats were often used for sport.

By 1920 the Mackinaw boat had almost disappeared from the Great Lakes. The last one in the Grand Traverse region was said to be owned by the Bunn Brothers of Elk Rapids. They were commercial fishermen around 1909 or 1910. Later they took the canvass off and installed a one-lunger gasoline engine.

Mackinaw boat owned and operated by Capt. Bonner of St. James, Beaver Island. He used it for trade with farmers and fishermen on other islands and the mainland.
LEELANAU COUNTY HISTORICAL SOCIETY

Mackinaw Boat at Leland Dock.
LEELANAU COUNTY HISTORICAL SOCIETY

Mackinaw boats used by fishermen.
MANITOWOC MARITIME MUSEUM

Two schooners, *John Mee* (at left) and *Ellen
Williams*, at Northport around 1895.
MANITOWOC MARITIME MUSEUM

4

Early Shipping

LaSalle's *Griffon* was followed first by a trickle, then — in the 1800s — by a flood of sailing ships on the Great Lakes. There were 407 of them in 1840, and by 1860 the number had grown to well over 1,000. They were all manner of craft — sloops, brigs, barks, brigantines and barkentines, as well as schooners and a few fully-rigged boats. Most of them were quite small, averaging about 115 tons, and by far the most numerous were the graceful, swallow-winged schooners, unrivalled on the Lakes for speed and maneuverability. In 1850, 80% of the sailing vessels on the Great Lakes were schooners; by 1870, the square-rigged ships had nearly disappeared.

The first half of the Nineteenth Century also marked the heyday of the great sidewheel steamers — ships like the *Great Western, Queen of the West, City of Buffalo, Iowa* and *Empire State* that carried the flood of immigrants from Buffalo to Chicago after the opening of the Erie Canal in 1825. (*Empire State,* one of the largest and most luxurious of the passenger steamers, sprang a leak in a storm on August 8, 1849, and was run aground by her captain on the beach south of Sleeping Bear. She was later released and resumed service until she was decommissioned in 1857. The town of Empire is said to be named after her, though others say that it was named after the schooner *Empire* that was ice-bound there in the winter of 1865.)

First of the side-wheelers on the Great Lakes west of Niagara was *Walk-in-the-Water;* she was named — so the story goes — after the startled exclamation of an Indian chief. Launched near Buffalo in 1818, she made a trip to Mackinac the following year, and, according to Henry Schoolcraft, was "much marvelled at" by the Indians there. In 1821 she went ashore off Buffalo in a storm and broke up; only her engine was salvaged.

The great increase in passenger traffic after the completion of the Canal created a demand for faster and more dependable transportation than sailing ships could provide. By the end of 1825, seven sidewheelers were making regular runs between Buffalo and Detroit. And by 1850, there were dozens of the big passenger steamers running from Buffalo and Detroit to Chicago.

The first side-wheeler to enter Grand Traverse Bay was the *Michigan,* in 1851. She was built at Detroit by Newberry and Dole, and launched in the spring of 1833. She was 156 feet long, 29 feet wide (53 feet over her paddle wheel guards) and 11 feet deep. She foundered somewhere in Lake Michigan on March 20, 1885. Paddle-wheelers plied the waters of the Bay as late as 1880. Among them were the *General Paine, A. H. VanRaalte, General Sheridan* and Dexter & Noble's *Queen of the Lakes.*

The first screw-driven steamers were fairly late-comers on the Great Lakes. Called "propellers" to distinguish them from the side-wheel steamers, they developed rapidly once their practicality was established. The first one on the Lakes — and probably the first commercial propeller in the world — was the *Vandalia,* 138 tons, built at Oswego in 1841. By 1860 there were still 139 side-wheel steamers in operation on the Lakes, but the number of propellers had increased to 197 and sailing vessels to 1122.

By far the busiest place in the Grand Traverse region during the 1840s and early '50s was South Manitou Island. Strategically located on the main waterway for traffic between Chicago and Milwaukee and Buffalo, its harbor was an invitation to passing ships. Even as late as 1902, when shipping on the Lakes was past its peak, over fifty ships of all kinds passed the Manitous in a single day. And during a gale it was not uncommon to see as many as fifty boats sheltering in South Manitou harbor.

South Manitou was the first wooding station in the Grand Traverse region, and one of the busiest on the Lakes. Until around 1880, when the conversion was made to coal, all the lake steamers used wood for fuel. The hard wood was cut into four-foot lengths, and split, and it sold in the early days for $1.50 to $2.00 a cord. The average steamer burned up about 150 cords of wood on a round trip from Buffalo to Chicago.

The first dock and wooding station on South Manitou was built by W. N. Burton between 1835 and 1838. Burton also served as the first lighthouse keeper on the island in 1840. Six years later, Nicholas Pickard and his brother Simeon, who had been in the wooding business in Erie County, N. Y., built a wooding dock on South Manitou Island. Other wooding stations were soon established at Glen Arbor, Glen Haven, Carp Lake (Leland) and Northport. At the height of this activity in the 1870s and '80s there were as many as 20 wooding stations along the Traverse region shoreline. Four of them were located at Northport, which by 1860 had become the main stopping point for steamers bound for Chicago and Buffalo.

Each of the Northport docks sold an estimated 35,000 cords of wood a year, along with food staples and such fresh provisions as fish and garden vegetables for the dining salons of the big passenger steamers.

In contrast to this bustling activity on the Manitous in the 1840s, the rest of the Grand Traverse region was almost an unbroken wilderness. Peter Doughtery's Indian Mission on the Peninsula had been established in 1839, but ships' captains were reluctant to enter the uncharted waters of Grand Traverse Bay, and it was visited regularly only by the schooner *Arrow* out of Mackinac and infrequently by small craft from the Manitou such as Captain Boardman's *Lady of the Lake*.

In 1847, Captain Harry Boardman, of Napierville, Ill. (he probably got his military title from service, along with the young Abraham Lincoln, in the Blackhawk Indian War of 1832) arrived at the present site of Traverse City in his little sloop *Lady of the Lake*. Also on board was Boardman's son Horace

Schooners at Peterson Mill dock, Suttons Bay, **about 1900.** CONRAD A. GRONSETH COLLECTION

6

Drawing of schooner *Madeline*.
TRAVERSE CITY PUBLIC LIBRARY

and two or three men, and some of the material for a sawmill, which they built that year on Mill Creek, later known as Asylum Creek and now Kid's Creek. While the mill was being built, *Lady of the Lake* made a trip to Manistee after plank for the flume. In October, while awaiting supplies at South Manitou Island, the little sloop was driven ashore in a gale and completely wrecked. Since there was no other vessel to take him back to the sawmill settlement, Captain Boardman had to take passage on a steamer to Mackinac, then cross to the mainland and hike back on foot along the lakeshore from the Straits, an exhausting journey of several days. The supplies were finally picked up and delivered by the schooner *Arrow*.

On June 11, 1849, the Chicago-built, two-masted schooner, *Hiram Merrill*, brought

Reverend George N. Smith and his party to Northport Harbor, where he established the first white settlement. His party consisted of two other white families and 50 Ottawa Indians, all from near Holland, Mich., where Smith had charge of an Indian mission.

In the spring of 1851, the three young men who were to found the Hannah, Lay & Co. lumber empire, arrived at Grand Traverse Bay aboard the little schooner *Venus*, after a tempestuous voyage from Chicago. They were Perry Hannah, Albert Tracy Lay and James Morgan. The *Venus* stopped first at Old Mission and stayed two hours, then set sail north for the western arm of Grand Traverse Bay. Off Old Mission Point, while the Captain was taking a well-earned nap, she struck a rocky reef and was held fast. Several hours later she was finally able to back off without much damage. Her Captain was Peter Nelson, who later served as lighthouse keeper for the Northport Light and for years was a resident of that village.

Another now-famous ship on the Bay in 1851 was the schooner *Madeline,* which spent the winter at Bowers Harbor. During that time the five members of the crew, uneducated men, hired an Old Mission resident, 19 year old S. Edwin Wait, to teach them to read and write. Regular classes were held aboard ship, and Wait received $20 per month and his board for his services. All six men went on to successful careers — the sailors as captains and lighthouse keepers on the Lakes, Wait as proprietor of Traverse City's Pioneer Drugs and one of the most highly respected and beloved of its citizens.

Other ships known to have sailed on the Bay in the early days — aside from the boats owned by or leased to Hannah, Lay & Co., which will be discussed in the next chapter — were these:

Prop. *Troy,* from Chicago and Grand Haven. Nov. 3, 1858, at TC.

Sch. *Eclipse,* Capt. J. W. Brown. June 10, 1859, at Traverse City.

Sch. *H. C. VanRaalte,* Capt. O. Evans. Regular runs in 1859 from Traverse City to Grand Haven, stopping at Elk Rapids, Northport, Manistee and Muskegon. She was crushed in the ice in East Bay on Mar. 23, 1860, and lost.

Sch. *Perry Hannah,* owned by Gray & Sims of Detroit; Capt. Canfield, formerly Capt. of the *Storm Spirit.* May 3, 1859, at TC.

Prop. *Mendota.* Sept. 23, 1859, at TC.

Sch. *Hamlet.* April 6, 1860 at Northport.

Schooner *Stafford* on west side of North Manitou near Crescent in 1909. Boat took on load of hemlock bark.
MICHIGAN STATE UNIVERSITY HISTORICAL COLLECTIONS

Three masted schooner.
LEELANAU COUNTY HISTORICAL SOCIETY

Prop. *Nile,* Capt. E. R. Collins. Stopping at Northport on regular run from Buffalo to Milwaukee and Chicago. 1860.

Sch. *Grape Shot.* Oct. 26, 1860, at TC.

Sch. *Amelia* struck by lightning in Grand Traverse Bay. July 13, 1862.

Sch. *Zephyr,* Capt. Eli Coon. Capsized in East Bay on April 19, 1862. Mess boy trapped in cabin but rescued by opening a hole in ship's bottom. No permanent damage to ship.

Sch's. *Denmark, Gypsy* and *Evelina.* May 2, 1862 at TC.

Bark *Winslow* and Sch. *Mann.* Nov. 28, 1862, at TC.

Prop. *Lady Franklin.* Dec. 5, 1862, at TC.

Sch. *Hiram Merrill* brought Rev. George N. Smith to Northport harbor on June 11, 1849.

Sch. *Susquehannah,* arrives with goods for Hulburd Bros. Sept. 1871.

Stm's. *Badger State, City of Traverse* and *Lawrence* waiting at Glen Arbor, *Wade* and *Metropolis* at Northport because clouds of smoke over land and water made navigation hazardous; Oct. 12, 1871. During this terribly dry year great forest fires raged in Michigan and Wisconsin, and Chicago burned down on October 8-9, 1871.

Stm's. *City of Traverse, Ella Burrows, Queen of the Lakes, East Saginaw, General Sheridan* and *Little Western* — 6 steamers all docked at Hannah, Lay wharf; July 26, 1872.

Sch. *David Stewart* at TC dock with 993 tons of iron rails for the GR&I railroad.

In addition to the boats listed above, there were many lake steamers that stopped at Northport and Glen Arbor, en route to

Frankfort. Mich. Sept 4th 1865.

Chicago, Detroit, Cleveland and Buffalo, during the late 1850s, '60s and '70s. Northport was a particularly busy port (much busier than Traverse City), logging 318 propellers in 1861, 328 in 1862, and 340 in 1863. Boats known to have stopped regularly at Northport and other Traverse region ports, during this period were these:

Propellers *Buckeye, Michigan, Ontario, Wisconsin, Empire, Ogdensburg, Prairie State, Champlain, Lawrence* and *Cleveland* —Northern Michigan Transportation Company. Regular run between Buffalo and Chicago.

Idaho, Fountain City, St. Lawrence, Arctic and *Oneida.* Western Transportation Company, New York Central Line. Buffalo to Chicago.

B. F. Wade, City of Fremont, Sun, Montgomery and *Dean Richmond.* Grand Trunk-Sarnia Line. Sarnia, Detroit, Mackinac, Milwaukee and Chicago.

Sch. *Clara Adams,* Capt. Charles Davidson. Dec. 9, 1862, in TC. Will lay up in Little Traverse for winter.

Sch. *Harriet Ross,* first ship to go ashore at Traverse City; mistook the light at Gunton House for the dock light. May 3, 1867.

Sch's. *Northport, Collingwood, Grape Shot* and *Ralph Campbell.* June 27, 1867, at Northport.

Ship loading lumber at East Head dock for Cobbs & Mitchell lumber mill on East Bay, 1890.
TRAVERSE CITY RECORD-EAGLE

10

Schooner *Belle.* MANITOWOC MARITIME MUSEUM

Bark *Three Bells,* dragged her anchor and went ashore near Hannah, Lay east wharf. Oct. 4, 1867.

Tug *G. W. Wood,* from Chicago, pulled off *Three Bells,* which sailed for Chicago loaded with lumber. Oct. 11, 1867.

Brig *Roscius* leaves for Chicago from TC loaded with lumber. Nov. 29, 1867.

Brig *Roscius,* last ship to leave TC in 1867, first to arrive in 1868. April, 1868.

Str. *Little Western,* owned by the Greilick Company, first steamer on the Boardman River. July 22, 1869.

Sch. *Kate Richmond* hard aground off Old Mission Point with cargo of wheat. Towed to Chicago. Nov. 11, 1869.

Sch. *Anne D. Hanson,* bark *Glenbeulah,* Sch. *William Crosthwaite* and brig *Orkney Lass* at TC. May 19, 1870.

Bark *LaFrainier* and sch. *Millard Filmore* ran aground at Traverse City. Towed off by str. *General Paine.* Nov. 17, 1870.

Prop. *Dictator,* with goods for Hulburd Bros., last boat in Traverse City for the season. Dec. 15, 1870.

Sch. *Kewaunee,* first arrival of season at TC. April 3, 1871.

Schooner at Suttons Bay 1890.
CONRAD A. GRONSETH COLLECTION

Two small steamers and schooner at Charlevoix harbor. PIONEER STUDY CENTER

Schooner. LEELANAU COUNTY HISTORICAL SOCIETY

Schooner *A. W. Lucky*, built 1867 at Detroit.
LEELANAU COUNTY HISTORICAL SOCIETY

Schooner *Cora A.* and tug *Watkins. Cora A.* built at
Manitowoc 1889. Lost in Atlantic March 6, 1916.
LEELANAU COUNTY HISTORICAL SOCIETY

Schooner *Ellen Williams*, built 1855 at Cleveland.
LEELANAU COUNTY HISTORICAL SOCIETY

Boats of Hannah, Lay & Company

The first Hannah, Lay sailing ship was the brig *J. Y. Scammon*. She was wrecked in the Manitou Passage in her first year of service, 1854. A year earlier, the company had purchased the *Telegraph*. She was a two-masted schooner of 267 tons, 117 feet long by 26 feet wide. In 1856, she was sold to her master Captain Ira Harrison and chartered to the Hannah, Lay company. She continued to haul lumber to Chicago at least until 1860, when on April 12 of that year she was reported to be the first arrival of the season at Traverse City; Perry Hannah was aboard.

Other ships sailing under lease to the Company were the schooners *Carrington, Main, Storm Spirit* and *Perry Hannah*. *Perry Hannah* first arrived at Traverse City on May 8, 1859, fresh from her launching on the St. Clair River in April. She was 98 feet long, 25 feet wide and of about 210 tons. Her skipper was Captain Canfield, who had been master of the *Storm Spirit*.

The first Hannah, Lay steamship was the propeller *Allegheny*. It was built at Milwaukee in 1854 for the American Transportation Company at a cost of $46,500. That company failed in the winter of 1858-'59, and the *Allegheny* was taken over by a Buffalo bank. It was purchased from the bank in 1860 by Hannah, Lay at a bargain $14,000, and in April of that year opened a regular run for freight and passengers between Traverse City and Chicago.

On April 28 she sailed on her first voyage with 300,000 feet of Hannah, Lay lumber and several passengers. One of them was Morgan Bates, editor and publisher of the *Grand Traverse Herald*.

"We have made the trip to Chicago and back on Hannah, Lay's propeller *Allegheny*," he reported a few weeks later. "She is as staunch, steady, safe and pleasant a boat as we have ever travelled on; her passenger accommodations are good, her table fare excellent, and her officers and crew cour-

Grand Traverse Herald, July 7, 1865.

teous and attentive. The trip to Chicago, instead of being a terror, dread and often a ten day voyage, as it was in sail vessels, is now a pleasant pastime."

Although, during her following ten years of service, the *Allegheny* and her dependable captain, C. H. Boynton, became dear to the hearts of Traverse area people, she was nevertheless an unlucky ship, forever getting into trouble.

Item: Serious accident off the Manitous, Sept. 20, 1860. She blew a cylinder and had to be towed to Northport. Delayed 3 weeks for repairs.

Item: Accident ten miles from Traverse City, Nov. 1, 1860. Broke connecting rod; came into port under sail.

Item: Oct. 10, 1862, *Allegheny* run into by brig on Lake Huron near Sarnia. Delayed at Chicago 8 weeks for repairs.

Item: May, 1864, *Allegheny* collides with schooner at Milwaukee. Schooner, laden with 19,000 bushels of oats, sunk; little damage to *Allegheny.*

Item: June, 1866, she broke her shaft and lost her wheel off Racine. *B. F. Wade* took her cargo and passengers to Northport. *Allegheny* towed to Chicago for repairs.

Item: Nov. 7, 1866, she broke another shaft 15 miles off Milwaukee. Tug *Achma* towed her into Milwaukee and brought her passengers to Northport. Perry Hannah was aboard and personally refunded all passage money.

Allegheny's doughty Capt. Boynton became seriously ill in the winter of 1866 and was replaced for the 1867 season and thence-forward by Captain George Baldwin. Despite her many mishaps, she was regarded as a faithful ship, and she continued in service for four more years, making weekly round trips to Chicago (and sometimes to Port Huron and Detroit), with stops at Frankfort, Carp River (Leland) and Northport. During her first six years she kept Traverse City people informed on the course of the Civil War by picking up the latest newspapers at Chicago and Detroit. Over the years she carried 72 million board feet of lumber for Hannah, Lay & Co., and 18 million shingles.

Her end was not dignified. Many a Traverse Citian wiped away a tear when it was announced in the *Herald,* in November 1870, that she had been sold and would be converted to a barge for service on Lake St. Clair. "Goodbye, *Allegheny,*" wrote editor D. C. Leach. (Incidentally, there is no connection between the old *Allegheny* and the Coast Guard tug of that name which served as a training ship for the Great Lakes Maritime Academy during the early 1970s; the tug got its name long before it was brought to Traverse City.)

City of Grand Rapids. LEELANAU COUNTY HISTORICAL SOCIETY

City of Traverse at Soo Locks.

Meanwhile, in 1864, Hannah, Lay & Co. had purchased the small steamer *Sunny Side* for service around Grand Traverse Bay. She was built at Detroit by Stewart McDonald at a cost of $13,000, and began regular trips around the Bay under Capt. Emory in the spring of 1865. Departing Traverse City at 7 a.m., she called at Elk Rapids, Antrim City, Pine River (Charlevoix), Old Mission, Bowers Harbor (Haight's dock) and Suttons Bay, returning to her berth at Traverse City every evening. She also ran excursions to Marion Island.

In 1866, she got new and spacious upper-deck cabins and a new Captain, John Drake. On November 22, 1867, she was totally wrecked at Pine River, driven against the wharf there by a gale and dashed to pieces. She was insured for only $5,000.

To replace the *Allegheny,* Hannah, Lay's elegant steamer, *City of Traverse,* was built by Quayle & Martin at Cleveland in 1870 at a cost of $85,000. Of 1200 tons, she was 225 feet long and 32 feet wide. She had luxurious accommodations for 75 passengers and could carry up to 640,000 board feet of lumber, three times as much as the *Allegheny.* When she arrived at Traverse City on May 4, 1871 on her maiden voyage, she was greeted by a large crowd of people, who went aboard to admire such splendid furnishings as her Brussels carpeting and black walnut furniture. Her captain was George Baldwin, last skipper of the *Allegheny* before its disposition, and her

TIME CARD

—OF THE—

Traverse City & Petoskey

STEAMBOAT LINE

For the Season of 1880.

STEAMER	STEAMER

CITY OF GRAND RAPIDS

WILL RUN NORTH

On Monays, Wednesdays & Fridays.

Leaving Traverse City	8.00	a. m.
" Old Mission	10.30	"
" Elk Rapids	11.15	"
" Torch Lake	1.00	p. m.
" Northport	2.20	"
" Norwood	4.00	"
" Charlevoix	5.30	"
" Petoskey	7.30	"
Arrive at Little Traverse	8.00	"

WILL RUN SOUTH

On Tuesdays, Thursdays & Saturdays.

Leaving Little Traverse	7.00	a. m.
" Petoskey	8.00	"
" Charlevoix	9.30	"
" Norwood	11.00	"
" Northport	12.15	p. m.
" Torch Lake	1.30	"
" Elk Rapids	3.00	"
" Old Mission	3.45	"
Arriving at Traverse City	6.30	"

O. E. WILBUR, Master.

CLARA BELLE

WILL RUN NORTH

On Tuesdays, Thursdays & Saturdays.

Leaving Traverse City	7.30	a. m.
" Old Mission	10.00	"
" Elk Rapids	11.00	"
" Torch Lake	1.00	p. m.
" Norwood	2.20	"
" Charlevoix	3.40	"
" Petoskey	7.00	"
Arriving at Little Traverse	7.30	"

WILL RUN SOUTH

On Mondays, Wednesdays & Fridays.

Leaving Little Traverse	7.00	a. m.
" Petoskey	8.00	"
" Charlevoix	9.30	"
" Norwood	11.30	"
" Torch Lake	12.45	p. m.
" Elk Rapids	2.15	"
" Old Mission	3.00	"
Arriving at Traverse City	6.30	"

A. G. ALDRICH, Master.

HANNAH, LAY & CO., Proprietors.

THE BEST PLACE TO HAVE YOUR

Fall and Winter

Grand Traverse Herald, October 1, 1880.

clerk and steward was S.E. Wait. The Cleveland *Plain Dealer* acclaimed her as "probably the best of her class on the Lakes."

She began her regular weekly run to Chicago in May, 1871. During her first year of service she made 23 trips to Chicago, carrying 12,639,950 feet of lumber. She also made three trips to Buffalo that year, carrying a total of over 200,000 bushels of oats; and a trip to Erie, Pa., with 69,413 bushels of oats. She brought to Traverse City some 60,000 bushels of grain and carried 1,040 passengers, 592 out and 448 in.

City of Traverse served the Company until 1887, when she was sold to the Graham & Morton Line for use between Chicago and Lake Superior ports. Her end was even more ignominious than that of the *Allegheny*. After passing through several other hands, she came under control of a Chicago gangster syndicate and was used as a gambling ship offshore of that city. Finally, she was left to disintegrate in the mud at Benton Harbor,

once again under Graham & Morton ownership. Her fate was recorded by a Chicago newspaper on Sept. 28, 1907:

"Drawn up at the end of the canal at Benton Harbor, Mich., its nose poking into the mud, her bow half concealed by the heavy growth of weeds on either side of the narrow channel, lies the good ship City of Traverse... *For two and a half years she was the principal actor in an extraordinary attempt on the part of Chicago gamblers to baffle the law by means of modern science. The big ship was rigged as a floating poolroom, equipped with a wireless telegraphic outfit and commissioned as a means of transmitting race track returns regardless of the police."*

Meanwhile, in 1875, the Hannah, Lay Company had commissioned the building of a handsome little steamer, *Clara Belle*, named after one of Perry Hannah's two daughters. Under the command of Capt. Oscar Wilbur, of Northport, she entered service on the Bay on June 30, 1876. She was 75 feet long, 16 feet abeam and 5 feet deep in the hold, with a capacity of 60 passengers.

Clara Belle. PIONEER STUDY CENTER

On her daily schedule she left Northport early every morning, stopped at New Mission (Omena), Suttons Bay and Bowers Harbor and arrived at Traverse City at 11 a.m. She left Traverse City at 2 p.m. and returned to Northport by the same route.

Clara Belle became a great favorite of Traverse people; she was much in demand for excursions and chartered parties, and was used often by Perry Hannah to entertain friends and business associates. She was sold in 1882 and ran for several seasons on Pine Lake (Lake Charlevoix).

The last two boats owned by Hannah, Lay & Co., which disposed of its lumber interests in 1886, were the *City of Grand Rapids,* put in service in 1879 and the *T. S. Faxton,* in 1880. Both boats were used on the Traverse City, Petoskey, Mackinac Daily Line. The *Faxton* was sold in 1887 and the *City of Grand Rapids* in 1888. On October 22, 1901, the *T. S. Faxton*

caught fire and burned to the water's edge at Marine City, Mich. The same fate happened to *City of Grand Rapids,* which burned at Lions Head on Georgian Bay, November 7, 1907.

City of Grand Rapids. LEELANAU COUNTY HISTORICAL SOCIETY

City of Grand Rapids, summer of 1892.
ELDEN DAME COLLECTION

Northport 1868. Stmrs. *Fountain City, Idaho* and *Sun. St. Louis* on the shoal.
MANITOWOC MARITIME MUSEUM

Idaho, New York Central & Hudson River Line.
MANITOWOC MARITIME MUSEUM

Early Steamers on the Bay

In 1868, four years before the first railroad reached Traverse City, people of the Traverse Bay area crossed a transportation threshold of sorts. On June 5, 1868, DeWitt C. Leach, editor and publisher of the *Grand Traverse Herald*, put it into words:

"Nothing shows more unmistakably the increase in population and business in the Grand Traverse region than the additions made to our facilities for travel and shipping.

"Our first visits to Traverse City (in the early 1860s) were made when a small sail boat, plying between here and Northport, and making trips only as business offered, was the only means of making the journey. Sometimes the trip was made in a few hours, and at others a day and a night were required.

"Four years ago, Hannah, Lay & Co. put the Propeller Sunny Side *on the Bay. It was thought doubtful whether even one small steamer would pay at that time. But business and travel increased as greater facilities were offered, and today we have on the Bay all the conveniences necessary for a large and increasing business.*

"The Propeller Allegheny *makes weekly trips to Chicago and back.*

"The Gen. Paine, *of which we have not before spoken, and of which we now take occasion to say, that she is a neat, staunch, swift craft, makes tri-weekly trips between Traverse City and Manistee.*

"The Burrows *and the* Belle *make daily trips around the Bay, one arriving here in the morning and the other in the afternoon. Once a week the* Burrows *extends her trip to Pine River.*

"Thus it can be seen that it is now easy to reach any point on the Bay, at any time, and without delay.

"As the country is constantly progressing, our facilities for travel will increase rather than diminish. We shall never go back to the days of sail boats and row boats, of long dreary trips to Northport working against wind and tide and hoping against hope. Those days are gone forever. Let them go. There was in them more romance than adventure."

In addition to the boats listed above, the Grand Trunk & Chicago's Sarnia Line in 1867 began operating five boats on a regular run between Chicago and Detroit, with a stop at Northport. They were the *B. F. Wade,* Capt. Archibald Gillies; *City of Fremont,* Capt. Morris

Empire State, NYC Line. MANITOWOC MARITIME MUSEUM

Barrett; the *Sun*, Capt. Robert A. Jones; the *Montgomery*, Capt. Robert Nicholson; and the *Dean Richmond* (which went on to Buffalo), Capt. J. P. Hodges.

The *Belle*, a small propeller of 237 tons, was operated by Englemann's Eastside Shore Line. In 1867 she began service between Traverse City and Manistee, touching at Northport, Carp River, Glen Arbor and Frankfort for passengers and freight. At Manistee she connected with the Englemann steamers *Messenger* and *J. Barber*, for all ports between that town, Grand Haven and Milwaukee.

The *Ella Burrows* was an independent boat, owned and captained by O. B. Burrows of Manistee. She operated on the Bay from 1868 to 1873, when she left for Cleveland for good.

In July 1868, *Gen. H. E. Paine*, a sidewheeler, was put on the Northport-Pine River run, stopping at Traverse City, Old Mission, Elk Rapids, and Norwood. She continued in service on the Bay until 1871, when she was replaced by another sidewheeler, *A. C. Van Raalte*, under Capt. George Perkins. The *Van Raalte*, however, left on June 8, 1871, to enter the fruit trade from St. Joseph to Chicago. She was replaced by the *General Sheridan*, also a paddle-wheeler, which arrived at Traverse City on July 15, 1871.

In this game of musical chairs, the *Van Raalte* returned to the Bay in 1874, replacing the *General Sheridan* in 1875. She continued operation on the Bay run until around 1880, stopping at Torch Lake for connections with the *Susquehannah* to Milwaukee; with *Queen of the Lakes* to Spencer Creek, Torch River and Elk Rapids; and at Traverse City with *City of Traverse* for Chicago.

Another ship, which operated on the Bay for several seasons beginning in 1870, was Englemann's propeller *Lake Breeze*. She ran regularly from Northport to Norwood, with stops at Antrim City, Brownstown, Elk Rapids, Old Mission and Traverse City. Also on the Bay in the 1870s was the Dexter & Noble steam yacht *Jennie A. Sutton*, which made two trips daily around East Bay beginning in June of 1872.

On May 21, 1874, the *Grand Traverse Herald* reported that these ships were docked at Traverse City; they were *City of Traverse, Huron, Van Raalte, Jennie Sutton, Crusader, Gen. Sheridan*; and sailboats *S. J. Holly* and *Kitty Fayette*.

In 1882, steam tonnage, which was then almost all oak propellers, came to equal sail tonnage. In the following decade, when iron and steel freighters and passenger boats came into general use, the sailing ships were reduced to hauling pulpwood and produce from points not served by the propellers or inaccessible to them. The last commercial sailing ship on the Lakes was the windjammer *Our Son*, which foundered in Lake Michigan off Sheboygan in a gale on September 26, 1930. She was carrying a load of pulpwood.

City of Collingwood, Canadian passenger steamer,
on Traverse Bay. LEELANAU COUNTY HISTORICAL SOCIETY

John R. Stirling, frequent visitor at Grand
Traverse Bay ports early 1900s.
ROBERT WHITE COLLECTION

Arthur Wait's water paddle machine on Boardman
River, early 1880s; Union Street bridge in background.
PIONEER STUDY CENTER

Boats of the Inland Waters

Queen of the Lakes

Largest and probably best loved of all the boats to ply the inland waterway known as "Chain o' Lakes", was Dexter & Noble's *Queen of the Lakes*. She was an iron side-wheeler with a length of 108 feet, 19 feet beam, and four and two-tenths depth of hull. She was built at Wyandotte in 1872 by Frank E. Kirby, who later designed the first cross-lake car ferries on the Great Lakes, as well as several passenger boats including *Greater Buffalo* and *Greater Detroit*.

In 1866 Dexter & Noble built a big general store at Elk Rapids. During the following decade it grossed somewhere in the neighborhood of $360,000 annually, and much of this business must have been attributable to the transportation provided by *Queen of the Lakes*. In this sparsely populated area, the *Queen* carried an astonishing 1,241 *paying* passengers for example, during the month of July, 1873. A time card published in the *Elk Rapids Progress* for the 1873 season gives a total time of five hours including stops for the 35-mile run from Torch Lake to Elk Rapids.

Until 1875 the *Queen* ran in the morning from Torch Lake or Eastport to Elk Rapids, making the return trip in the afternoon. A year or two later, the schedule was reversed and she was berthed at Elk Rapids. During the spring and fall, when business was slow, she made only one-way trips each day, going up one day and coming down the next. When berthed at Elk Rapids, she was available for excursions and moonlight cruises, which became very popular on the Bay.

In spite of having been designed for shallow waters, the *Queen's* size made her awkward and hard to handle in the narrow and winding Torch River. Her speed, too, left something to be desired. In an effort to improve her speed and power, her deck was raised 18 inches in 1887 so as to reduce the dip of her paddles — but the change does not seem to have helped very much.

In 1881 the steamer *Ida* was put in service running from Elk Rapids to Bellaire, and it soon became apparent that this vessel together with the *Jennie Silkman* and other smaller craft were better suited for the winding small rivers.

Accordingly, the *Queen* was taken off the Chain o' Lakes run and in 1884 was sold to Captain Joseph Lloyd of Duluth, Minnesota. In June of that year, Capt. Lloyd arrived with a crew to take over the *Queen*, but the deal fell through in a dispute over financial details and he returned to Duluth without her. That season she made an excursion or two to

Charlevoix for Dexter & Noble and was finally sent there for operation on Pine Lake for the rest of the year.

In June of 1886 the sale of the *Queen* to Capt. Lloyd was finally consumated, and she was taken to Duluth for service on the Duluth to Superior run. Her new owner, however, found her unsuitable for this work and she was returned to her original owners that same month. On June 18, 1886, the *Elk Rapids Progress* reprinted the following item from the *L'Anse Sentinel:* "Queen of the Lakes has been found unfit for work on the Duluth Superior Line."

"Slight mistake," said the *Progress,* haughtily. "The work was not fit for the *Queen.*"

Other work was soon found for the *Queen.* Early in July she was sent south to run on Black Lake (now called Macatawa Lake, site of Holland, Mich.), where she operated under charter to the Chicago and West Michigan Railroad in competition with the steamer *Macatawa.* The latter boat was operated by

Queen of the Lakes at Noble & Dexter Elk Rapids store. July 17, 1867. NATALIE KOHLER COLLECTION

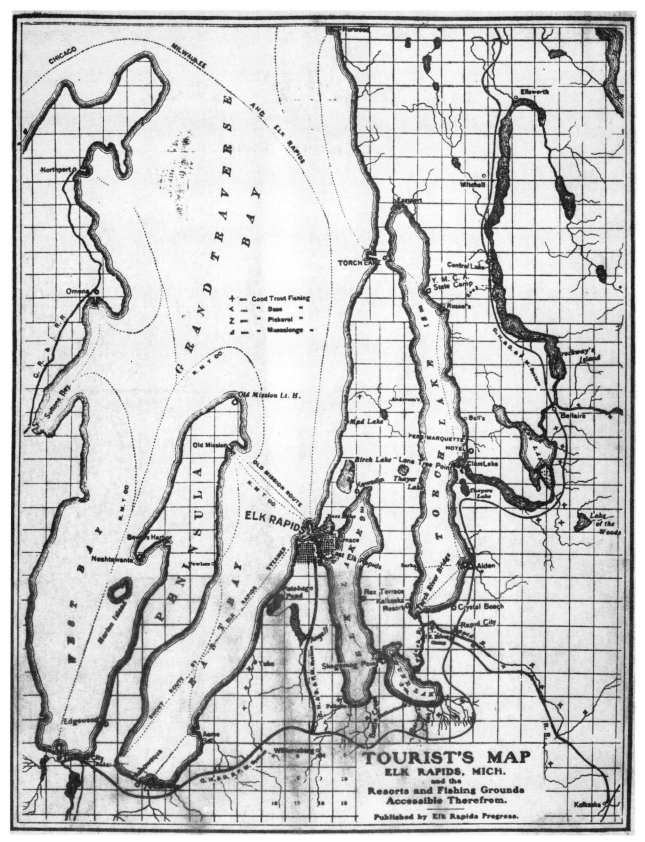

TOURIST'S MAP
ELK RAPIDS, MICH.
and the
Resorts and Fishing Grounds
Accessible Therefrom.

Published by Elk Rapids Progress.

NATALIE KOHLER COLLECTION

the owners of a summer resort, Macatawa Park, and until the *Queen's* arrival had enjoyed a monopoly. The *Queen's* efforts to break the monopoly led to a series of violent confrontations, legal and otherwise, which became known in the region as the "Steamboat War". The *Queen* finally won the legal battle and operated successfully for the rest of the season. At the end of the season she returned to Elk Rapids to lay up for the winter. For the next few years she continued to operate on Black Lake.

In 1894 she was sold to Alice E. Shipman of Escanaba to run between that place and Gladstone. Due to a breach of contract by Mrs. Shipman, she was returned to Elk Rapids and her original owners the following year.

In June of 1898, Captain Frederick Johnson, who had commanded the *Queen* throughout her entire career, bought her from the Elk Rapids Iron Company. Johnson took her to Grand Haven for fitting out and repairs, in anticipation of using her for excursions out

of Petoskey, Bay View, East Jordan and Charlevoix. On September 18, while returning to Grand Haven after the season's operations, she caught fire a half-mile from South Manitou, and burned to the water's edge. Exit *Queen of the Lakes,* the only iron ship ever to ply the Inland Waters.

Other Dexter & Noble Boats

The first sailing vessel of Dexter & Noble was the *Kingfisher*. She served the company until 1873, when she was abandoned in Clam River. The first steamer was the *Albatross*, a paddle-wheel tug built in 1864. While anchored in Elk Lake for the winter, on December 12, 1873 she was driven out on the lake in a gale and sunk. Refloated in 1874, she served only until 1875, when she was condemned. Her machinery was removed and installed in the Elk Rapids brickyard.

In 1871 the *Jennie A. Sutton* was built for the Company at Buffalo. She was a wooden side-wheeler of 301 gross tons. She served

Queen of the Lakes at Elk Rapids dock.

30

Tug *Torch Lake* with rafts loaded with cordwood
for iron furnaces. Wanigan at right was a
mobile, floating lumber camp.

first on the Inland Lakes and later sailed regularly around the Bay. She was 46 feet long, ten feet, four inches wide.

Dexter & Noble constructed its first blast furnace in 1873, and that same year built the *Torch Lake* to haul wood fuel for the smelting operation. She was a twin-screw tug, 57 feet long by 15 wide. During part of her career she bore the carved figure of an Indian with fully drawn bow atop her pilothouse.

Elk Lake, built by the Company in 1877, was very similar to *Torch Lake.* She was painted red and sported a pair of elk horns on her pilothouse, reportedly the same pair found by Abram Wadsworth at the mouth of Elk River for which the town and the river were named.

Third and last of the trio of tugs was the new *Albatross,* built at Buffalo in 1879. Not to be outdone by her sisters, she was painted white and had a carved, spread-wing albatross adorning her wheel house.

In addition to its other boats, Dexter & Noble had a fleet of 21 scows in 1873, and fifteen years later there were 28. All were about 60′x18′x45″ deep and could carry 35-40 cords of wood. In 1886 the iron furnace was consuming 36,000 cords of wood each year. The scows were all built in the Dexter & Noble shipyards. An exception was the steam scow, *Frank H. Petrie,* purchased in 1880 and dismantled in the winter of 1882-1883.

In 1884, the *City of Cheboygan* was purchased for use mainly as a transfer boat. She was an 85-by 17-foot side-wheeler, built at Cheboygan in 1880. In 1887 she was hauled into Elk River and fitted out with new iron wheels and wooden paddles. During the next several years she was used on the inland lakes to haul scows and also log rafts with as much as one million board feet of timber.

The assets of the iron company were purchased in 1907 by the Lake Superior Iron & Chemical Company. The *Albatross* continued in service until 1916.

Other boats that sailed on the Chain o' Lakes were the *Jennie Silkman,* named after

Dexter & Noble iron furnace and chemical plant at Elk Rapids. Steamer *Ruth* at dock.
NATALIE KOHLER COLLECTION

the wife of J. H. Silkman, who had a sawmill at Torch Lake; the tugs, *Little Western, Maple Leaf, Wahwahtopee, Goose* and *Mahsahmagosas,* whose name was changed in 1883 to *Bellaire* because her Indian name was too long to fit on a boat; the small steamers *Time* and *Grass Lake,* and the paddle-wheelers *Valley Queen* and *Lizzie Rose.* All were under other ownership than Dexter & Noble's.

The *Jennie Silkman* was built in 1882. This double-decker propeller made regular trips from Elk Rapids to Eastport, first as a passenger steamer and then as a tug for the Cameron Lumber Company, owners of the craft. There is an interesting footnote to her history. In August of 1940, Dan Berg, veteran boat man and dock builder of Clam River, salvaged the 500-pound propeller of the *Jennie Silkman* while making preparations to build a dock at Torch Lake village.

Steamers on Lake Leelanau

The first commercial passenger boat on Lake Leelanau (then Carp Lake) was probably the little steamer *Sally.* She began operating in the spring of 1892 under her

Steamer *Ruth* at Clam River.
NATALIE KOHLER COLLECTION

Schooners at Elk Rapids. NATALIE KOHLER COLLECTION

Ruth at **Skegemog Point.** NATALIE KOHLER COLLECTION

Mabel at Skegemog Point. NATALIE KOHLER COLLECTION

Queen of the Lakes on Grand Traverse Bay.
TRAVERSE CITY PUBLIC LIBRARY

master Morgan Cummings, who had been employed at the Leland Iron Company. She made one round trip each day between Leland and Fouch (where she made connections with the newly arrived Manistee & Northeastern Railroad), with stops at Provemont (Lake Leelanau) and Bingham Landing. Leelanau County people could meet the M&NE in the morning, spend seven hours in Traverse City, and catch the *Sally* homeward in the late afternoon. *Sally* was also available for charter fishing trips on the lake.

About 1894, the small steamer *Tiger*, under Captain John Hartung, took the *Sally's* place on Carp Lake, following the same schedule as her predecessor.

In 1900, Louis Mosier, owner of Mosier's Mill, built the steam propeller *Leelanau* with the help of his two sons, Leo and Joe. Designed by Louis Hockstead of Bingham, she was 68 feet, ten inches long and 15 feet abeam. She was built of heavy tamarack planking and a 6" x 6" rock elm frame. Her ribs were cooked in open-air kettles and bent to shape by hand. Her practically new engine and boiler were taken from the steamer *Ransom*, which had been brought from Buffalo, a year or two previously, by Louis Mosier and Morgan Cummings. In competition with the *Tiger*, the *Leelanau* began operating on Lake Leelanau in 1901.

An intense rivalry between the two boats led to a price war which, over the next couple of years, reduced the round-trip fare from $1.50 to $1.00 and then to 75¢. The time card for both vessels called for two round trips

Steamer Tiger,

low **Making Regular Trips**

—ON—

Carp Lake.

JOHN HARTUNG, Master.

Leelanau Enterprise 1894. Steamer *Tiger* had to lower its smokestack to clear the bridge at Provemont.

36

Steamer *Leelanau.* SLEEPING BEAR DUNES NATIONAL PARK

daily, one in the morning and one in the afternoon. Between Leland and Fouch the boats made stops at Provemont, Fountain Point, Horton's, Bingham Landing and Noland's.

The *Leelanau* was successful in driving the older *Tiger* off the lake, but on August 16, 1908, she met with tragedy. Just off Bingham Landing her vertical boiler blew up with a terrific roar. The blast threw passenger Mrs. Isabelle LaBonte overboard; her body was not found until five days later. It was ironic that John Hartung, former captain of the *Tiger* (he had sold her to Bernie Pickard for use as a tug on Lake Michigan) was at the wheel of the *Leelanau* when the explosion occurred. He was severely scalded by steam and boiling water and died a few days later at Munson Hospital.

Interviewed by an *Evening Record* reporter, owner Charles Mosier said he believed that a flaw in the dome of the boiler caused the explosion. Somewhat defensively he added, "Does anyone think that if I imagined there was a chance of the boiler going up that I would sit day after day right over it for hours at a time? I think too much of my wife and babies for anything like that."

After lying at Bingham Landing for some time, the *Leelanau* was sold to John VerSnyder. He installed a new engine and boiler and continued to operate her on Lake Leelanau until 1929, when ill health forced him to retire. It is said that VerSnyder beached the boat near his home, raked the coals out from under her boiler, and never set foot on her again. He died a short time later at Munson Hospital.

The *Leelanau* was left to disintegrate slowly in the mud. Her boiler is said to have been taken to Traverse City for use by the Grand Traverse Metal Casket Company. Some of the timber from her hull and pilothouse reportedly went into a house on the Wilburt Gauthier farm three miles south of the village of Lake Leelanau.

Another small steamer, *Carrie Palmer,* made regular trips between Leland and Provemont for a season or two beginning in 1909. She was owned and commanded by Charles Mosier.

Aboard the *Lou Cummings.*
LEELANAU COUNTY HISTORICAL SOCIETY

Lou A. Cummings, Traverse Bay Line.

Traverse Bay Boats

In 1887 Captain Henry Webb bought a half interest in the small steamer *Onekama* from the Seymour Brothers in Manistee and launched the Traverse Bay Line. Under the command of Captain Joe Emory, who owned the other half interest in the boat, the *Onekama* opened a regular schedule in 1888, running from Northport to Traverse City, with stops at Bowers Harbor and Suttons Bay.

Webb, who began his career as a druggist in his home town of Cassopolis, Mich., owned a cottage at Neahtawanta Point and had been spending his summers there since 1870. In 1889, he bought the *Lou A. Cummings* and put her on the Traverse City-East Jordan run, following the same schedule as had the *Sunny Side*. Webb took control of the line in 1900 and had the *Crescent* built at Grand Haven at a cost of $75,000. She replaced the *Onekama* on the Northport-Traverse City run, while the latter was used for two or three years for daily round trips between Old Mission and Elk Rapids.

In 1892, the *Columbia* was built and added to the fleet. Webb sold his interest in the *Onekama* to Capt. Emory in 1894, and for the next ten years the three small steamers, *Lou Cummings*, *Crescent* and *Columbia*, made their regular trips around the Bay. After the turn of the century, however, the railroads (particularly the TCL&M) cut sharply into the business, and the fortunes of the Traverse Bay Line entered a steep decline.

The *Lou Cummings* was sold in 1905, the *Crescent* in 1906, and the *Columbia* in 1907. Captain Webb died in January of 1906, and his interests were taken over by his son, Captain Charles Webb. With the sale of the *Columbia*, people of the Grand Traverse region for the first time in almost 40 years were left without transportation on the Bay.

To rectify this situation, a group of Traverse City people got together in 1906 and formed the Traverse Bay Transportation Company. They were Charles Webb, A. V. Friedrich, Anthony Greilick and his son Frank, Elsie Hannah, R. Floyd Clinch and Sam Garland. For $28,000 they bought the steamer *Chequamegon* from the Northern Transportation Co. She was greeted upon her arrival at Traverse City on June 12, 1907, by the blowing of all the factory whistles in town. Members of the company had gone to Ludington to make the maiden trip to Traverse City.

The *Chequamegon* forthwith began her daily run from Traverse City to Charlevoix, touching at Bassett Island, Neahtawanta, Omena and Northport. She left Traverse City at 8 in the morning and returned at 7 p.m. Charles Webb was her skipper and Frank Greilick her chief engineer.

In 1906 the company had purchased Bassett Island, the tiny island off the northeast end of Marion Island, and built a 250-foot dock, bathhouses and a 100' x 50' dancing pavillion there. Both the *Columbia* and the *Chequamegon*

Lou A. Cummings. LEELANAU COUNTY HISTORICAL SOCIETY

ran evening excursions to the island. Passengers had a full two hours for dancing and refreshments before returning to Traverse City. The ballroom was on the upper level of the pavilion, kitchen and dining room on the lower level. Jesse Tallerday, former wheelsman of the *Columbia*, was in charge of the Island enterprise. A fellow townsman of Captain Henry Webb's at Cassopolis, Tallerday was jocularly known as "Robinson Crusoe". One of the first moving pictures shown in the area was screened at Bassett Island on July 27, 1907. Passengers had the option of watching it from the steamer decks or from seats on the dock. Electricity was supplied by the steamer dynamo.

The *Chequamegon* was considered one of the finest small steamers on the Lakes. She was built in 1903 by the president of the Northern Transportation Co., for his son, and she was used on a run between Milwaukee and Whitefish Bay, where the Pabst beer people had built a big resort. Later, a trolley was built from the railroad to the resort, cutting into the *Chequamegon's* business, and she was put up for sale. She was slightly over 100 feet long, with a capacity of about 500 passengers. Her upper deck had a ladies' cabin fitted out in antique oak; so was the men's cabin on the lower deck. Below and forward was a spacious dining saloon.

Her only serious mishap occurred near Northport on August 16, 1909. Her cook, Bert Silver, lost his balance and fell overboard while heaving a bucket of slops into the water, and drowned.

Under an arrangement with Northern Transportation Company, passengers from Chicago to Traverse City could transfer from the *Manitou* at Charlevoix and be carried to Traverse City on the *Chequamegon* at no additional fare. A deal was also made with the Northern — and with the Manistee & Northeastern Railroad — to pick up fruit in season at various ports around the Bay. During the course of her career the *Chequamegon* also

made several wildcat runs to High Island and the Foxes for loads of shingles.

Other small boats on the Bay at this time were the *Fannie Rose* under Captain Emory, and, for a season or two, B. F. Lardie's *Lena Knoblock*. In 1909, for example, the *Chequamegon* was serving the west shore towns on the Bay, the *Fannie Rose* making regular round trips between Traverse City and Neahtawanta, and the *Knoblock* plying between Old Mission, Bowers Harbor and Traverse City.

That year the *Fannie Rose* dropped off a load of horses at Marion Island for Birney Morgan, following an old practice used formerly by Old Mission farmers to graze horses and pigs on the island for the summer. The practice had been discontinued after a few years because the Indians — so the farmers complained — were helping themselves to the young porkers. The horses were unloaded offshore and had to swim to the Island.

The era of regular transportation on the Bay came virtually to an end in 1911, when

Lou A. Cummings at Bassett Island.

Northport 1890s. Left to right, *Emma Thompson, Columbia, City of Grand Rapids, Alice M. Gill, City of Charlevoix.* At rear, *Lawrence.* ELDEN DAME COLLECTION

Lou A. Cummings and *Illinois* at Traverse City
Docks. PIONEER STUDY CENTER

Columbia. PIONEER STUDY CENTER

Chequamegon
ROBERT WHITE COLLECTION

Columbia, Grand Rapids
and *Lou A. Cummings* at
unidentified dock.
LEELANAU COUNTY HISTORICAL SOCIETY

Steamer *Crescent* at Northport dock.
ELDEN DAME COLLECTION

the *Chequamegon* was sold to the Pere Marquette line of steamers for the run between Pentwater and Ludington. The *Fannie Rose* continued to run on the Bay waters until around 1914. The dance pavillion on Bassett Island was sold in 1934 to W. R. Foote, owner of the Grand Traverse Auto Company, and torn down for the lumber.

Fruit Boats on the Bay

Cherries had been grown in the Traverse region almost from the beginning. But the first orchard on a grand scale was planted near Northport in 1912-1913. Francis H. Haserot, a wholesale grocer of Cleveland who had been spending his summers at Northport for many years, finished planting 14,000 Montmorency cherry trees in 1913; the orchard became known far and wide as Cherry Home.

In 1916 Haserot built a cannery and a dock on the Bay just north of Northport. In addition to its own fruit, Cherry Home also processed cherries from other orchards in the region, and from the first there was a "cherry boat" picking up cherries at ports around the Bay.

One of the first boats chartered by the Company was the *Schnoder* whose home port was St. James on Beaver Island. Later, the factory had its own boat, the *Gilman D.* She was built in 1921 by Isa Dame, a brother of Gilman M. Dame, who was manager of the factory. Nicknamed "Bull Moose", the *Gilman D.* was steam powered with a coal-fired water tube boiler and a triple expansion engine. Later it was converted to diesel.

Before the season, the cherry boat ferried supplies — fuel, cans, sugar, etc., — from the railroad at Northport. After the close of the canning season it made trips down the Lakes to Cleveland and Chicago with the product of the factory.

During the season, the boat made daily trips to Old Mission to bring back the day's pick. The arrival of the "Bull Moose", heavily laden with cherries from across the Bay, was the big event each evening at the cannery during the processing season.

By the late 1920s, so many orchards had come into production that Cherry Home was no longer able to process all the fruit available. In 1929, a large new cannery was built in the village of Northport, between the railroad and the old carferry dock, and the old factory at Cherry Home was dismantled. In 1946, the *Gilman D.* was sold for use on Saginaw Bay.

Meanwhile, the John C. Morgan Canning Company of Traverse City had begun to operate fruit boats on the Bay. The principal product of the Morgan cannery was apples, and around 1915 the *Anna C. Wilson* was picking up apples around the Bay and in Wisconsin for the Morgan Transportation Company, a subsidiary of the canning company. She soon became known as the "apple boat".

In 1922, the *Wilson* was replaced by the *Mary Ethel.* Originally a schooner, the *Mary Ethel* had been converted to steam in 1916. She continued to bring apples to the Morgan cannery until the late 1920s. Her Captain was Don S. Morgan. In November of 1927 she brought a load of apples to the cannery from Sturgeon Bay and the Manitou Islands.

Another boat that supplied the Morgan factory with apples was the *Stewart.* On November 7, 1927, she had a run-in with the *Manitou.* She was unloading apples at the *Manitou's* side of the Traverse City dock when the *Manitou* herself nosed in out of the mist, towering above the *Stewart* like a leviathon. Captain Walter Petroskey of the *Manitou* got on the bull horn and demanded that the Stewart move out of the way to the other side of the dock. The Stewart's captain had gone downtown, and her crew continued impassively to unload apples as though they were deaf. It finally took Eli Weston, local agent for the Northern Transportation Company, to persuade the crew of the *Stewart*

Chequamegon at Traverse City.

to move over. Captain Petroskey had yelled himself hoarse to no avail.

That same year, the *Mary Ethel* and the *Stewart* had brought 70,000 bushels of apples to the Morgan cannery from Sturgeon Bay and the Grand Traverse region ports.

In October of 1933, Traverse Bay cherries were shipped by water for the first time to the East Coast. The Federal Motorship Corporation's *Buckeye State* loaded 20 carloads of canned cherries at the Traverse City dock for shipment to New York and Philadelphia by way of the Welland Canal, the New State Barge Canal, and the Hudson River.

Crescent on Grand Traverse Bay.

Columbia. PIONEER STUDY CENTER

46

Crescent. ELDEN DAME COLLECTION

Lena Knoblock. PIONEER STUDY CENTER

B. F. Lardie's *Lena Knoblock.* PIONEER STUDY CENTER

GUYLES DAME COLLECTION

LEITNER,   Photo

Wm. Gill & Son, Gill's Pier, Mich.
DEALERS IN
Hardwood Lumber, Cordwood, Bark, Ties and Posts by the Cargo.

Suttons Bay waterfront 1890s. Coal dock, Bahle dock, Peterson dock and Deuster dock. Boat at Bahle dock (front) is the *Sylvia*. Second boat may be the *Eva Hill*. CONRAD A. GRONSETH COLLECTION

Fannie M. Rose loading potatoes at Bowers Harbor. EDWARD BARDY COLLECTION

Schnoder at Cherry Home dock.
CONRAD A. GRONSETH COLLECTION

Cherry Home warehouse & dock.
CONRAD A. GRONSETH COLLECTION

Northern Michigan Transportation Company

Since the 1850s the Northern Transportation Company had been serving Chicago, Buffalo and many ports between, including Ludington, Manistee, Frankfort, Glen Haven, Petoskey, Harbor Springs and St. Ignace. On some of its schedules regular calls were also made at Traverse City, Suttons Bay, Omena, Northport and Old Mission.

In 1893 there were two competitive lines operating regularly scheduled steamers to the places listed above — the Seymour Transportation Company and the Northern Transportation Company. The Seymour Line was owned by three Seymour brothers of Manistee. The latter company was managed and partly owned by Simeon S. Burke of Chicago.

The Seymour Line had two ships, the *Puritan* and the *Petoskey*. Acquired from the Morton Transit Company, the *Puritan* had been built in Benton Harbor in 1887; she was 171 feet long and 28 feet abeam. The Petoskey was of the same length but a little broader in beam; she was built at Manitowoc in 1888. The skipper of the Petoskey in 1893 was Captain William Robertson. He was followed in later years by Captain Peter Kilty, whose fate it was to go down with his ship, the car ferry *Pere Marquette 18,* when she foundered in a gale on Lake Michigan on September 8, 1910, with a loss of 28 lives.

The Northern Michigan Transportation Company also had two ships, the *Lawrence* and the *City of Charlevoix.* The *Lawrence,* a small vessel, had been built in Cleveland in 1868; she was 135 feet long by 26 wide. The *City of Charlevoix* was also built at Cleveland, two years later. She was slightly larger than the *Lawrence,* 165 feet by 28. Originally called the *Champlain,* she was captained in 1893 by William Finucan and her purser was Eli A. Weston, a Traverse City man who later became the local agent here for the Company.

Grand Traverse Herald, July 30, 1891.

In 1887, the *Champlain* became the instrument of a tragedy.

The Burning of the Champlain

Approaching midnight, June 17, 1887. A mild star-lit night on Grand Traverse Bay. The steamer *Champlain*, having departed Traverse City at 5:00 p.m. and stopped briefly at Norwood, is running on schedule just off Fisherman's Island, also called Little Island, six miles south of her destination at Charlevoix. 57 passengers and crewmen are aboard. Captain Edward Casey, a veteran seaman of the Lakes, is on the bridge.

Suddenly, terrified shrieks rend the calm of the night. Engineer McCaffery bursts on deck with his clothing aflame. Screaming horribly, he dashes to the hurricane deck and dives into an open tank of water kept there for emergency purposes. McCaffery is followed on deck by the assistant engineer and the firemen, all yelling that the engine room is in flames. Roused by the commotion, the passengers pour from the cabin doors. Smoke and flames are already rising from around the stack and the after-cabin. Within a few moments all is panic and confusion.

All, that is, except Captain Casey. He keeps a cool head. He orders the engine-room crew back down to shut off the power and drop headway so that the lifeboats can be lowered. Several make the attempt but are forced back by the flames. By this time the whole aft end of the ship is on fire. The two forward life boats are lowered, but they are swamped as the ship's speed continues unabated. As a last resort, the Captain orders the wheel swung hard-a-port to bring the ship as close as possible to the island.

Meanwhile, the passengers have been milling around on deck in panic, screaming and praying as the flames drive them forward. The crew has thrown overboard everything that will float—doors, fenders, life preservers.

City of Charlevoix **at Northport.** ELDEN DAME COLLECTION

Str. Champlain at Charlevoix Pier
Burned At Fishermans - Island June 17, 1887
22 Lives Lost.
Thomas Friant Petoskey Str.
coming in.

PIONEER STUDY CENTER

Passengers and crew have rushed for the life-jackets, but many of them are ill-adjusted or merely carried in hand. Soon, the flames force passengers and crew to jump into the chill water. About 37 of them (the number is uncertain) eventually reach shore on the island, swimming or hanging onto anything afloat. 21 persons lose their lives.

Among them were an Indian and his three sons, and 15 passengers and crew members who were never identified. All were buried in a cemetery at Charlevoix with simple headstones bearing only numbers.

Also among them was Mrs. Mary Kehoe of Chicago. She jumped carrying her baby in her arms. Mrs. Kehoe was not seen again, but her close friend, Mary Wakefield of Traverse City, who had jumped simultaneously, took the baby's clothing in her teeth and swam to shore at Fisherman's Island and safety. She was acclaimed a heroine of the sad affair.

The *Champlain* went aground about a mile from the island. There was a lumber camp there and a tug sent out by the lumbermen was able to pick up several of the survivors. A telephone line from the lumber camp to Charlevoix brought medical help to the burned and injured.

As the search went on for survivors and bodies, a tug from Charlevoix put a line aboard the burning ship and towed her to the south pier, where the fire was finally extinguished. The cause of the fire was a kerosene lamp which fell to the floor in a fireman's cabin and burst into flames. The fire spread immediately to oily rags and other debris in the engine room. Engineer McCaffery eventually recovered from his burns.

Although the *Champlain* had burned almost to the water's edge, she was later rebuilt as the *City of Charlevoix* and continued to serve for many years in the freight and passenger trade. In her latter years of service she was named the *Kansas*.

In 1895 the Seymour Line and the Northern Michigan were merged, the newly formed company retaining the latter name. The old

53

Lawrence. LEELANAU COUNTY HISTORICAL SOCIETY

Lawrence 1885. MANITOWOC MARITIME MUSEUM

Puritan and the *Lawrence* were eliminated and only the *Petoskey* and the *City of Charlevoix* were kept in service. The *Puritan* operated for a time between Manistee and Milwaukee, then was laid up in Manistee Lake, where later she was destroyed by fire. The *Lawrence* was placed in year around operation between Muskegon and Milwaukee.

In the latter 1890s both the *Petoskey* and the *City of Charlevoix* called regularly at Traverse Bay ports on their run between Chicago and Mackinac Island. Their schedule included stops at Frankfort, South Manitou, Glen Haven, Glen Arbor, Leland, Northport, Omena, Suttons Bay and Traverse City.

The Company launched a new steamer, *Illinois*, in April of 1899. She was a beautifully appointed ship, said to be the finest on the Lakes. She was 225 feet long by 40 feet

wide, with a capacity of 1,500 tons of freight and luxurious accommodations for 250 passengers.

Built at Chicago at a cost of $250,000, she replaced the *Petoskey*, which was sold to the Hart Line of Green Bay. The *Petoskey* finally burned at Manitowoc, where she had been built so many years before. Captain of the Illinois was William Finucan and her purser, Eli Weston.

The *Illinois* was joined by a sister ship, the *Missouri*, in 1904. She was also built at Chicago and was of the same dimensions as the *Illinois*. William Finucan brought her out from Chicago on her maiden voyage; he was succeeded on the bridge of the *Illinois* by Capt. "Bud" Richardson.

Her arrival at Traverse City on April 19, 1908 — as the first ship of the season — was

Puritan. LEELANAU COUNTY HISTORICAL SOCIETY

Kansas, formerly City of Charlevoix. TRAVERSE CITY PUBLIC LIBRARY

City of Charlevoix. ELDEN DAME COLLECTION

City of Charlevoix. LEELANAU COUNTY HISTORICAL SOCIETY

recorded eloquently by the *Record-Eagle*:

Like a phantom ship coming out of the mist, the steamer Missouri *glided into the Bay at 8 o'clock this morning, making scarcely a ripple on the placid water, and formally opened navigation at Traverse City. The big steamer received a hearty welcome not only by the crowds who stood on the dock awaiting her arrival, but her whistle was replied to by whistles from the factories and mills.*

An even more luxurious ship, the *Manitou*, was added to the fleet in 1906, purchased from the Manitou Steamship Company. Built at Chicago in 1893, she was 274 feet long and 42 feet wide. With a top speed of 19.5 miles per hour, she was said to be one of the fastest ships on the Lakes. Captain William Bright sailed her for her original

owners and was relieved by William Finucan at the time of her purchase, Bright replacing Finucan on the bridge of the *Missouri*. The *Missouri* later came under the command of Captain George Johnson of Traverse City, who had been skipper of the *Kansas*.

An additional purchase in 1912 brought a newer and larger *Puritan* to the line. She was acquired from the Graham and Morton Transportation Company and had been built in Toledo in 1901. Her captain was "Jack" Crawford.

All four of these fine ships — *Illinois, Missouri, Manitou* and *Puritan* — for many years became familiar but always exciting sights on Grand Traverse Bay. Over the years they carried thousands of horses to the Grand Traverse region, returning to Chicago

North Union Street, Traverse City, early 1900s.
Puritan offshore.

with thousands of bushels of potatoes and shiploads of canned cherries.

The advent of the automobile and the motor truck spelled the doom of the great Lake Michigan passenger boats just as surely as they replaced the horse and buggy. With the coming of the War in 1917, the *Manitou* and the *Puritan* were requisitioned by the United States government, but were returned to their owners in 1919, having seen little or no service in the conflict. The Seymour brothers sold their interests in the Northern Michigan Transportation Company to Judge Robert W. Dunn of Chicago, and the line was henceforth known as the Michigan Transit Company.

In 1927, R. Floyd Clinch bought the *Puritan* and the *Manitou* for $102,000 and $125,000 respectively. He also assumed obligation for $100,000 worth of claims against the ailing Transit Company. The sister ships, *Illinois* and *Missouri*, were taken over by the Wisconsin & Michigan Line and for a number of years ran year around between Muskegon and Milwaukee.

Clinch was the son-in-law of A. Tracy Lay, one of the principal partners in Hannah, Lay & Company, and he had extensive business interests and land holdings in Traverse City. Under his ownership the *Puritan* and the *Manitou* continued to make regular calls at Traverse Bay ports, but the company became insolvent in 1931 and operations were abandoned.

This, for all practical purposes, marked the end of regular passenger service on Bay waters. Henceforth, the only large ships to be seen on Grand Traverse Bay were the oil tankers, coal and chemical boats, and an occasional cruise ship of the Georgian Bay Line — *North American, South American* and *Alabama* — which went out of business in 1967. (In May of 1937, the *John J. Boland*, largest ship ever to enter Grand Traverse Bay up to that time, brought a load of coal to Traverse City.)

Missouri. ELDEN DAME COLLECTION

58

Northport early 1900s. From left, *Charlevoix*,
Manistique car ferry and *Manitou*.
ELDEN DAME COLLECTION

Petoskey at its launching at Manitowoc in 1880.
MANITOWOC MARITIME MUSEUM

Petoskey. LEELANAU COUNTY HISTORICAL SOCIETY

Petoskey. LEELANAU COUNTY HISTORICAL SOCIETY

In 1933 an attempt was made to restore the *Manitou* and the *Puritan* to Lake Michigan passenger service. Purchased by the newly formed Isle Royale Transit Company, the *Manitou* was renamed *Isle Royale,* and the *Puritan* renamed the *George M. Cox,* after the president of the new company.

The *Isle Royale* was in operation only during the season of 1933, carrying cruise passengers from Chicago to Isle Royale and other Lake Superior ports. On September 13 of that year her crew threatened to scuttle her at Chicago, claiming non-payment of back wages, and a Federal judge ordered the ship seized by U.. S. marshals. "Mutiny on the Manitou", the *Record-Eagle* called it, lamenting the fate of a "once proud ship". In the following year, while laid up in Manistee Lake, she was seriously damaged by fire. Her charred hulk was sold in 1935, and later she was reduced to a barge.

The *George M. Cox* had a more spectacular end; it came on May 27, 1933.

The Sinking of the Cox

John F. Soldenski, keeper of the Rock of Ages Light off the southern end of Isle Royale, couldn't believe his eyes. A few minutes before, from his perch atop the 11-story lighthouse, he had seen the twin masts of a ship rising above the fog. Now slowly they turned until they were lined up on a collision course with the lighthouse. Soldenski frantically sounded the fog whistle as a big ship loomed larger and larger out of the fog . . . .

The *George M. Cox,* formerly *Puritan,* left Chicago on her inaugural trip on the Chicago-Isle Royale passenger run with only 18 passengers. She looked brand spanking new, with a new coat of white paint for her hull and one of black for her stack, and on, her upper deck, new staterooms, cabins and other accommodations had been built. She sailed under the command of Captain George E. Johnson, veteran lake skipper from Traverse City. The 18 passengers were enjoying a free ride at the invitation of their friend, George

Puritan - Cox.

E. Cox of New Orleans, who was also aboard.

On June 27, 1933, at about 2 p.m., the *Cox* left Houghton and steamed to the western end of the waterway that bisects the base of the Keweenaw peninsula. Entering Lake Superior again, the Captain set her course for the Rock of Ages Light, intending to turn there to starboard for the run to Fort William, where 250 passengers were waiting to be picked up. Captain Johnson put the first mate in charge and went below. The *Cox* proceeded smoothly at 17 knots on a gently undulating sea covered with patches of fog.

Around 6:30, just after some of the passengers had been seated for the evening meal, there was a heavy thud followed by a series of crashes. China plates and crystal goblets flew through the air and shattered, together with trays of food. Furniture and dining passengers slid down the floor and crashed into the bulkhead. Passengers in their cabins fell down, got up and fell down again. "What happened? What happened?" people cried as they rushed out on the tilted deck.

What happened was that the *Cox* had struck the rock reef between the Rock of Ages Light and the channel buoy. The shock was so great that her engines were torn loose from their foundations. The ship's bow was high on the reef and out of water, while her aft end was awash and she was listing 40 degrees to port. The radio operator banged out SOS signals.

Because of the list it was impossible to lower the starboard lifeboats, but those on port were successfully launched and they carried all the passengers and crew to safety at the Lighthouse. There they spent a wretched night huddled around the base of the Light. The lighthouse was too small to accommodate all of them, so they had to take turns going inside to get warm. Early next morning they were taken aboard the Coast Guard cutter *Crawford* and carried to Houghton. (Summoned by the SOS, the *Crawford*

had sped to the scene during the night from her base at Two Harbors, Minn.) Altogether, the *Cox's* crew had transferred 120 people from the wreck: the largest mass rescue in Lake Superior history.

The cause of the wreck was never satisfactorily explained. A court of inquiry absolved Captain Johnson of negligence but censured the first mate, who, the Captain claimed, had steered the wrong course: NW½N instead of the given NW¼N. The mate vehemently denied it, but several members of the crew corroborated the Captain's testimony.

A Thunder Bay tug removed all the personal belongings of the passengers and crew, and other things moveable including two new 1933 automobiles belonging to George Cox; but, during the next few weeks, the wreck was picked clean of everything else of value by local fishermen and scavengers. The remains of the ship broke in two during an October storm and slid off the reef into deeper water. Today the *Cox* is part of the Isle Royale National Park and off limits to skin divers.

Captain Johnson retired from the Lakes after the loss of the *Cox*. Until his death in 1948 he served as register of deeds for Grand Traverse County. His friend, Eli Weston, who was local agent for the Northern Michigan Line, died two years later. Both men are buried in Oakwood Cemetery in Traverse City.

The great days of the schooners and passenger steamers are gone forever. But today, after all those years, the Bay is filled with sails again. Sailing for sport and pleasure has become more popular than ever, and it seems safe to say that, as long as the waters of Grand Traverse Bay endure, there will always be boats upon it, of one kind or another.

Lawrence. LEELANAU COUNTY HISTORICAL SOCIETY

Illinois & Columbia. Traverse City, Mich.

Illinois. PIONEER STUDY CENTER

City of Charlevoix. PIONEER STUDY CENTER

Illinois. PIONEER STUDY CENTER

SUMMER SCHEDULE

SEASON 1904

STEAMSHIP "ILLINOIS"

GOING NORTH

Lv. Chicago................every Tue. at 1.00 pm
" Ludington............ " Wed. " 1.30 am
" Manistee............. " " " 4.30 am
" Frankfort............ " " " 8.30 am
" Glen Haven.......... " " " 11.30 am
" Glen Arbor.......... " " " 12.00 n'n
" Charlevoix.......... " " " 5.30 pm
" Petoskey............ " " " 8.00 pm
Ar. Harbor Springs...... " " " 8.30 pm

GOING SOUTH

Lv. Harbor Springs.......every Wed.at 10.00 pm
" Traverse City........ " Thur. " 6.00 am
" Omena............. " " " 7.30 am
" Northport........... " " " 8.30 am
" Frankfort........... " " " 3.00 pm
" Manistee............ " " " 6.30 pm
" Ludington........... " " " 10.00 pm
Ar. Chicago............ " Fri. " 9.00 am

GOING NORTH

Lv. Chicago............every Fri. at 7.00 pm
" Ludington............ " Sat. " 8.00 am
" Manistee............ " " " 11.00 am
" Frankfort........... " " " 3.00 pm
" Glen Haven.......... " " " 6.00 pm
" Glen Arbor.......... " " " 6.30 pm
" Northport........... " " " 10.30 pm
" Elk Rapids.......... " Sun. " 4.00 am
" Old Mission......... " " " 5.00 am
" Traverse City........ " " " 8.00 am
" Charlevoix.......... " " " 12.30 n'n
" Petoskey............ " " " 3.00 pm
Ar. Harbor Springs...... " " " 3.30 pm

GOING SOUTH

Lv. Harbor Springs.......every Sun. at 4.00 pm
" Petoskey............ " " " 5.00 pm
" Charlevoix.......... " " " 6.30 pm
Ar. Traverse City........ " " " 10.00 pm
Lv. Traverse City........ " " " 12.00 n't
" Elk Rapids.......... " Mon. " 3.00 am
" Old Mission......... " " " 4.00 am
" Northport........... " " " 6.00 am
" Frankfort........... " " " 12.30 n'n
" Manistee............ " " " 3.00 pm
" Ludington.......... " " " 6.00 pm
Ar. Chicago............ " Tue. " 6.30 am

STEAMSHIP "KANSAS"

In Commission July 1 to October 1

GOING NORTH

Lv. Chicago.............every Mon. at 7.00 pm
" Pentwater............ " Tues. " 7.00 am
" Ludington........... " " " 8.30 am
Ar. Manistee............ " " " 11.00 am

GOING SOUTH

Lv. Manistee ....every Wed. at 3.00 pm
" Ludington .... " " " 6.00 pm
" Pentwater .... " " " 7.30 pm
Ar. Chicago .... " Thur. " 7.30 am

GOING NORTH

Lv. Chicago ....every Thur. at 7.00 pm
" Pentwater .... " Fri. " 7.00 am
" Ludington.. .... " " " 8.30 am
Ar. Manistee............ " " " 11.00 am

GOING SOUTH

Lv. Manistee.............every Fri. at 3.00 pm
" Ludington .... " " " 6.00 pm
" Pentwater .... " " " 7.30 pm
Ar. Chicago .... " Sat. " 7.30 am

GOING NORTH

Lv. Chicago ....every Sat. at 3.00 pm
" Pentwater .... " Sun. " 3.00 am
" Ludington .... " " " 4.30 am
Ar. Manistee .... " " " 7.00 am

GOING SOUTH

Lv. Manistee.............every Sun. at 3.00 pm
" Ludington.. .... " " " 6.00 pm
" Pentwater .... " " " 7.30 pm
Ar. Chicago .... " Mon. " 7.30 am

STEAMSHIP "MISSOURI"

GOING NORTH

Lv. Chicago ....every Wed. at 1.00 pm
" Ludington............ " Thur. " 12.30 am
" Manistee............ " " " 3.30 am
" Charlevoix .... " " " 12.30 n'n
" Petoskey............ " " " 3.00 pm
" Harbor Springs....... " " " 4.00 pm
Ar. Mackinac Island.... . " " " 8.00 pm

GOING SOUTH

Lv. Mackinac Island......every Thur.at 9.00 pm
" Cheboygan .... " " " 11.00 pm
" Harbor Springs....... " Fri. " 6.00 am
" Petoskey............ " " " 7.00 am
" Charlevoix .... " " " 9.00 am
" N. Manitou Island.... " " " 12.00 n'n
" Glen Arbor.......... " " " 12.30 pm
" Glen Haven.......... " " " 1.00 pm
Ar. Chicago .... " Sat. " 6.30 am

GOING NORTH

Lv. Chicago ....every Sat. at 7.00 pm
" Ludington............ " Sun. " 6.30 am
" Manistee............ " " " 9.00 am
" N. Manitou Island .... " " " 2.00 pm
" Charlevoix ... . " " " 6.30 pm
" Petoskey............ " " " 8.30 pm
" Harbor Springs....... " " " 9.30 pm
" St. Ignace............ " Mon. " ... am
" Cheboygan .... " " " 4.00 am
Ar. Mackinac Island...... " " " 6.30 am

GOING SOUTH

Lv. Mackinac Island......every Mon. at 8.00 pm
" Cheboygan (via Ferry) " " " .... pm
" St. Ignace........... " " " .... pm
" Harbor Springs....... " Tues. " 6.00 am
" Petoskey............ " " " 7.00 am
" Charlevoix .... " " " 9.00 am
" Manistee............ " " " 4.00 pm
" Ludington........... " " " 7.30 pm
Ar. Chicago .... " Wed. " 6.30 am

Local Passenger Rates Tourist Season 1904

CHICAGO AND MILWAUKEE TO

LUDINGTON (Meals and berth extra).....	Cabin, One Way........$2.50 / Cabin, Round Trip..... 4.00	ELK RAPIDS	Cabin, One Way......... $ 7.00 / Cabin, Round Trip.... 13.00
MANISTEE (Meals and berth extra)........	Cabin, One Way....... 2.50 / Cabin, Round Trip..... 4.00	CHARLEVOIX	Cabin, One Way........ 8.50 / Cabin, Round Trip..... 15.00
FRANKFORT...........................	Cabin, One Way....... 5.50 / Cabin, Round Trip....10.00	PETOSKEY	Cabin, One Way........ 8.50 / Cabin, Round Trip.....15.00
GLEN HAVEN...........................	Cabin, One Way....... 7.00 / Cabin, Round Trip.....13.00	BAY VIEW................	Cabin, One Way........ 8.50 / Cabin, Round Trip.....15.00
GLEN ARBOR	Cabin, One Way....... 7.00 / Cabin, Round Trip.....13.00	WE-QUE-TON-SING	Cabin, One Way........ 8.50 / Cabin, Round Trip.....15.00
NORTH MANITOU	Cabin, One Way....... 8.00 / Cabin, Round Trip.....14.00	HARBOR POINT	Cabin, One Way........ 8.50 / Cabin, Round Trip.....15.00
NORTHPORT	Cabin, One Way....... 7.00 / Cabin, Round Trip.....13.00	ROARING BROOK	Cabin, One Way........ 8.50 / Cabin, Round Trip.....15.00
OMENA	Cabin, One Way....... 7.00 / Cabin, Round Trip.....13.00	HARBOR SPRINGS...........	Cabin, One Way........ 8.50 / Cabin, Round Trip.....15.00
SUTTON'S BAY	Cabin, One Way....... 7.00 / Cabin, Round Trip.....13.00	ST. IGNACE.	Cabin, One Way........ 9.50 / Cabin, Round Trip.....17.00
TRAVERSE CITY	Cabin, One Way....... 7.00 / Cabin, Round Trip.....13.00	MACKINAC ISLAND	Cabin, One Way ...... 9.50 / Cabin, Round Trip.....17.00
OLD MISSION	Cabin, One Way....... 7.00 / Cabin, Round Trip.....13.00	CHEBOYGAN	Cabin, One Way ...... 9.50 / Cabin, Round Trip.....17.00

MEALS AND BERTH INCLUDED IN CABIN PASSAGE, EXCEPT TO LUDINGTON AND MANISTEE.

We are the only line out of Chicago landing passengers direct at Petoskey.

OUR HOTEL LIST

TOWN	HOTEL	RATE PER DAY	RATE PER WEEK	CAPACITY
Ludington	The Sterns	$2.00 to $2.50	Special	250
	Hotel Russell	2.00	Special	75
	Hotel Epworth	2.00	$ 8.00 to $10.00	300
	Read	2.00	10.00 to 12.00	50
Manistee	Dunham	2.00 to 2.50	....	200
	The Buckner	1.00	....	....
	The Marion	1.50	6.00	....
Frankfort	Hotel Frontenac	3.00 to 4.00	Special	500
	Pere Marquette	2.00	10.00 to 12.00	150
	Parker House	1.00	5.00 to 7.00	50
	Park House	2.00	5.00 to 8.00	150
Glen Haven	Sleeping Bear House	1.25	6.00	....
Northport	Cedar Lodge	2.00	....	....
	Northport Beach Hotel	3.00 to 5.00	14.00 to 28.00	250
	Scott Hotel	2.00	....	....
	Wilson Cottage	1.00	....	....
Omena	The Leelanau	2.50	8.00 to 14.00	200
	Omena Inn	2.00 to 2.50	Special	150
Traverse City	Park Place	2.00 to 3.00	....	150
	Whiting	1.50 to 2.00	....	150
	The Columbia	1.50	....	....
Elk Rapids	Lake View House	2.00	10.00	....
	Riverside Hotel	1.50 to 2.50	Special	....
Charlevoix	Charlevoix Inn	3.00 to 4.00	14.00 to 21.00	700
	Chicago Club House	2.00 to 4.00	12.00 to 15.00	300
	The Belvidere	2.00 to 3.00	10.00 to 12.00	600
	New Bartlett	2.00 to 3.00	7.00 to 10.00	150
	Ferguson House	1.50	5.00 to 8.00	75
	Beach Hotel	2.00 to 3.00	Special	....
	Hotel Elston	2.00 to 3.00	"	....
St. James	The Beaver	2.00	....	....
	The Gibson House	2.00	....	....
Old Mission	Stone	1.00	6.00	25
	Old Mission House	1.50	7.00	35
	Old Mission Inn	1.50	7.00	50
	The Pines	2.00	10.00	....

Illinois, October 28, 1908. PIONEER STUDY CENTER

MISSOURI AT N. M. T. CO'S DOCK, TRAVERSE CITY, MICH.

12298 Cabin of Steamer Missouri of Northern Transportation Co.

Missouri and *Chequamegon* at Traverse City.
PIONEER STUDY CENTER

Missouri at Northport, early 1900s.
ELDEN DAME COLLECTION

ELDEN DAME COLLECTION

70

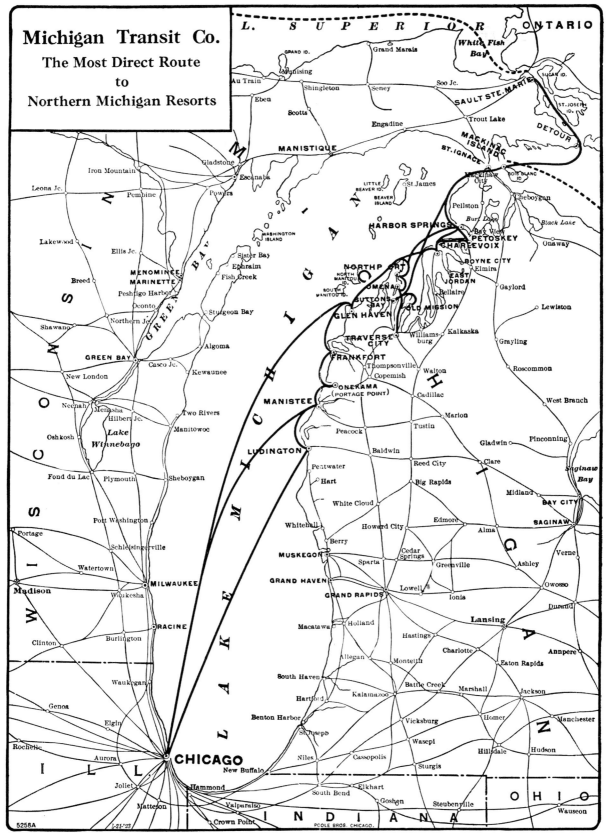

Michigan Transit Co.
The Most Direct Route
to
Northern Michigan Resorts

71

Shipwrecks of the Traverse Region

Travelling by ship on the Great Lakes in the early days was a dangerous business, not to be taken lightly. It was particularly hazardous in the spring and fall, when great storms lash the lakes into a frenzy. In 1869, for example, ninety-seven ships were lost in a four-day hurricane that swept the lakes clear. In 1880, the great gale of October 15 and 16 took a toll of 188 lives and almost 100 vessels. (The steamer *Alpena* went to the bottom somewhere off Grand Haven in that blow, with heavy loss of life. So did the schooner *J. H. Hartson* off Frankfort, with a load of iron ore.) Between 1878 and 1898, almost 6,000 vessels foundered on the Great Lakes. Other great storms on the Lakes occurred in 1905, 1913 and 1940.

In the Grand Traverse region, the waters of narrow Manitou Passage, with its treacherous sand shoals and rocky reefs, are especially dangerous. The Passage is a ships' graveyard, littered with the bones of old sailing ships and steamers. Most recent victim was the *Francisco Morazan* of Liberian registry, out of Chicago for Rotterdam, with a cargo of canned chicken, hides and gilsenite. She foundered off the south end of South Manitou Island in the big storm of November 30, 1960, and now lies broken-backed offshore with only her forecastle and stern still above water.

For almost a hundred years ships were guided through the Manitou Passage by the great South Manitou Light, one of the oldest on the Great Lakes. It was built in 1858 to take the place of the wooden structure which had been erected in 1839. Abandoned in 1929, it was replaced first by the lightship

Manitou Passage. Lithograph in Castelnau's *Vues et Souvenirs*, 1842.
SLEEPING BEAR DUNES NATIONAL PARK

Manitou (later re-named *Huron*), then by a fixed station known as the "Crib", in 21 feet of water on the North Manitou Shoals. The "Crib" is manned by a Coast Guard crew of five during the shipping season. It is scheduled to be replaced by a permanent automatic light in 1980.

The following, in chronological order, is a partial list of shipwrecks in the Grand Traverse region, as substantiated by at least two documentary sources. It is probable that at least as many wrecks went unrecorded.

Sloop *Lady of the Lake*, wrecked off the Manitous, Oct. 14, 1847.

Sch. *Black Hawk*, Nov. 1847, cargo of iron rails, disappeared off Frankfort with all hands.

Sch. *Energy*, 1854, household goods, foundered off Old Mission Point.

Str. *Westmorland*, 1854, misc. & gold, foundered off Empire, with 17 lives lost.

Brig. *J. Y. Scammon*, 1854, mixed cargo, Manitou Passage.

Str. *General Taylor*, 1855, foundered off the Manitous.

Str. *Brunswick*, Aug. 9, 1856, off South Manitou.

Sch. *Van Raalte*, March 1860, crushed in ice in East Bay; total loss.

Sch. *Leander Choate*, 1860, misc. cargo, off Northport harbor.

Sch. *Clara Adams*, Dec. 28, 1864.

Sch. *John Thursby*, 1867, fine china, off Ne-ah-ta-wanta Point in West Grand Traverse Bay.

Str. *Sunny Side*, Nov. 14, 1867, wrecked at Pine River (Charlevoix) dock.

Sch. *Equator*, 1869, railroad ties, stranded off N. Manitou.

Sch. *C. H. Herd*, 27,000 bu. of corn, off S. Manitou; 11 lives lost.

Bark. *Badger State,* 1871, wrecked off Sleeping Bear, cargo of corn.

Sch. *Gold Hunter,* 187?, off Glen Haven, china.

Sch. *Galena,* 1872, foundered off Lee's Point in West Bay.

Str. *Mendota,* Sept. 10, 1875, foundered off the Manitous, 12 lives lost.

Sch. *J. W. Hutchinson,* 1875, off South Manitou.

Sch. *Atlanta,* 1878, off South Manitou.

Sch. *W. B. Phelps,* Nov. 1879, wheat and bottled beer, 36 qts. to the case, off Sleeping Bear.

Sch. *Two Fannies,* Nov. 1879, stranded off Elk Rapids.

Sch. *W. B. Allen,* 1879, off South Manitou.

Sch. *Bangalore,* 1879, off South Manitou.

Str. *Fanny Hazelton,* Oct. 14, 1880, off Northport Point, telephone poles.

Sch. *Gertrude,* 1881, marble, off Empire.

Sch. *W. W. Brigham,* 1881, off the Manitous.

Str. *Columbia,* Sept. 10, 1881, off Frankfort, mixed cargo.

Sch. *James Platt,* spring 1882, 3500 barrels of salt, on South Fox.

Sch. *City of Green Bay,* same storm 1882, lumber, on South Fox.

Sch. *Potomac,* 1883, lost off Frankfort, beer.

Sch. *Guiding Star,* 1884, lost off the Manitous.

Str. *Jarvis Lord,* 1885, coal, foundered off the Manitous.

Sch. *Dickinson,* Nov. 1886, off Frankfort.

Sch. *Elgin,* 1886, off the Manitous.

Sch. *Hercules,* 1886, off North Manitou.

Sch. *Metropolis,* 1886, off Old Mission Point.

Sch. *Jessie Scarth,* Oct. 1887, east of North Manitou.

Josephine Dresden wrecked at North Manitou Island, November 27, 1907.
EMPIRE TOWNSHIP HERITAGE GROUP

Str. *Waverly,* 1887, off the Manitous.

Sch. *Niagara,* Sept. 7, 1887, foundered off the Manitous.

Sch. *Pulaski,* Oct. 3, 1887, foundered off North Manitou.

Sch. *R. M. Rice,* Oct. 3, 1888, stranded north of the Manitous.

Str. *Solon H. Johnson,* Oct. 1888, stranded off North Manitou.

Sch. *Ketcham,* 1890, off Lee's point.

Sch. *Brick,* 1891, machinery, foundered in East Bay.

Tug *Onward,* 1892, off Traverse City.

Sch. *Ostrich,* Oct., 28, 1892, off the Manitous.

Str. *W. H. Gilcher,* Oct. 28, 1892, disappeared off North Manitou.

Str. *Queen of the Lakes,* Sept. 18, 1898, ballast, burned to water's edge off South Manitou.

Sch. *Len Higby,* Oct. 1898, foundered off Frankfort.

Sch. *Templeton,* 190?, 350 barrels of whiskey, off South Manitou.

Sch. *Vega,* Nov. 28, 1905, off South Fox.

Sch. *H. D. Moore,* Sept. 10, 1907, stranded off South Manitou.

Sch. *Seaman,* 1909, lumber, off Sleeping Bear.

Schooner *Seaman* wrecked 1909 off Sleeping Bear Dune. PIONEER STUDY CENTER

Rising Sun, owned by House of David at Benton
Harbor. Built at Marine City 1888.
LEELANAU COUNTY HISTORICAL SOCIETY

Rising Sun, wrecked Oct. 29, 1917, off Pyramid
Point. SLEEPING BEAR DUNES NATIONAL PARK

Sch. *J. B. Newland,* Sept. 8, 1910, off North Manitou.

Str. *Bethlehem,* Sept. 23, 1910, flour and general merchandise, Manitou Passage.

Str. *Three Brothers,* Sept. 27, 1911, lumber, stranded off South Manitou.

Str. *David Z. Norton,* Oct. 7, 1912, wrecked off Sleeping Bear.

Str. *Rising Sun,* Oct. 29, 1917, stranded off Pyramid Point.

Str. *P. J. Rolph,* Sept. 8, 1924, foundered off South Manitou.

Str. *C. E. Redfern,* Sept. 19, 1937, pulpwood, off Point Betsie.

Motorship *Steelvendor,* Sept. 3, 1942, steel billets, Manitou Passage.

Str. *Francisco Morazan,* Nov. 30, 1960, off South Manitou.

One of the most bizarre sinkings in modern times happened in the Manitou Passage on September 3, 1942. The *Steelvendor,* southbound with a cargo of steel billets, ran into heavy seas east of the Manitou Islands. The steel motorship 258 feet long by 43 feet wide, developed a severe list and subsequent flooding of her after-end that prevented the crew from reaching the controls of her diesel engine to halt her. After circling out of control for more than two hours, while other vessels stood helplessly by, the crew abandoned ship at 3:45 in the morning, just six minutes before she sank. All hands were saved.

Schooner *Quick Step,* wrecked off Pt. Betsie, Oct. 1, 1912.

Walter L. Frost, wooden steamer built 1883 at
Detroit, stranded off South Manitou in dense
fog, Nov. 4, 1903, with cargo of corn.
SLEEPING BEAR DUNES NATIONAL PARK

Francisco Morazan, wrecked Nov. 1960, off South
Manitou. LEELANAU COUNTY HISTORICAL SOCIETY

South American.

Alabama. SLEEPING BEAR DUNES NATIONAL PARK

Whaleback freighter *Meteor* delivered gas and
heating oil to Greilickville dock in the 1950s.
PIONEER STUDY CENTER

Amoco *Indiana* at Greilickville 1979. Her sister
ships also calling at Traverse City are *Illinois* and
Wisconsin. JOHN RUSSELL PHOTO

Indian Trails, Wilderness Roads & Stagecoaches

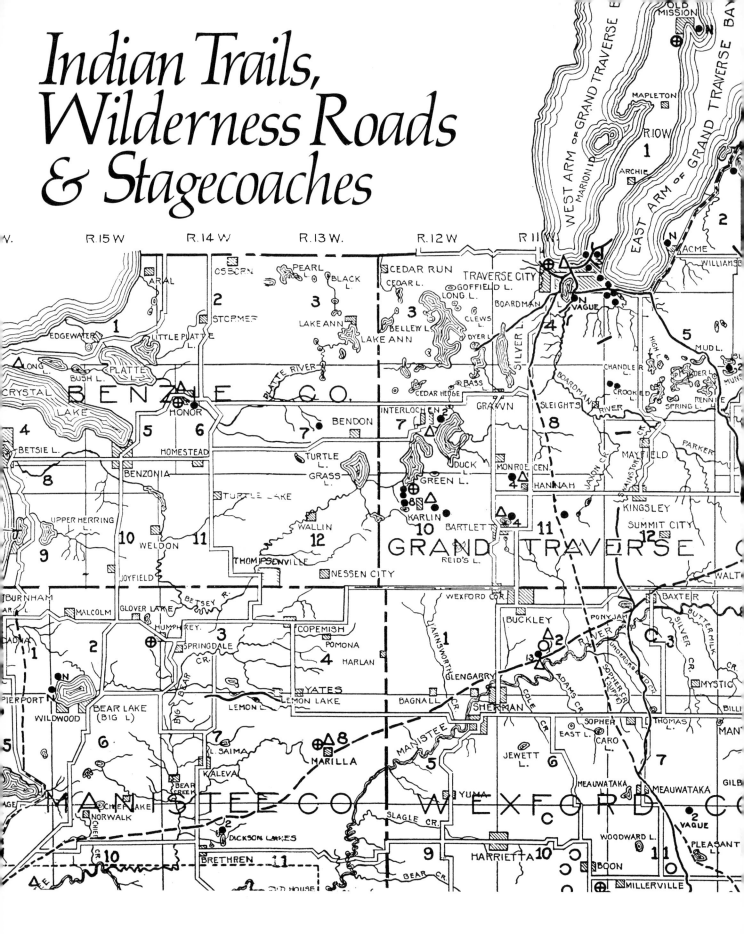

Indian Trails

It is difficult for us now, in these days of instant communications and jet travel, to realize how isolated the Grand Traverse settlement was in its early days. Perhaps that isolation is best illustrated by the following article which appeared in the *Grand Traverse Herald* on July 15, 1859:

How to Get to Grand Traverse

We received many letters from different parts of the country asking how people can get to Grand Traverse County.

To which we reply: Those living south or east will take a propeller at Buffalo, Dunkirk, Cleveland or Detroit, and come directly to Northport, which is situated on Grand Traverse Bay ten miles from its mouth. The fare from Buffalo to Northport is about $8 and from Detroit $5. Those who wish to visit the western part of the county on the shore of Lake Michigan will take a propeller which will agree to land them at Glen Lake or Leland.

Those coming from the west will take passage on one of the Hannah, Lay & Co. vessels at Chicago which sail regularly between that port and Traverse City during the season of navigation, or one of Noble & Dexter's, which will land them at Elk Rapids on the eastern shore of Grand Traverse Bay at the mouth of Elk River. The fare from Chicago to Traverse City by sail vessel is $5. There are small boats running regularly between Northport, Traverse City, Elk Rapids and the Mission, which will take passengers to any point on the Bay.

There is no land route to this place except by Indian trail, on which the mail is brought once a week. In winter this is our only route to the outside world. A route for a State Road through the wilderness from Grand Traverse Bay to Charlevoix has been surveyed this season, and the time is not far distant when we shall have a good thoroughfare to Grand Rapids.

Editors with whom we exchange will confer a favor by copying the above.

From *Archeological Atlas of Michigan*, Walter B. Hinsdale. Ann Arbor 1931.

For almost fifteen years, from 1850 through the early sixties, Traverse City people were completely isolated from the rest of the world during the four or five months when winter closed down all navigation on the Great Lakes. Perry Hannah, who served a term in the state legislature in 1856-1857, had to travel to Lansing on foot accompanied by an Indian guide. Because of heavy snow they were able to manage only ten or twelve miles a day, camping out in the woods at night, and it took them the best part of two weeks to make the journey.

That, of course, was the way the Indians had been getting around for hundreds, even thousands of years. Through a network of well-marked trails they were able to communicate and trade with one another from one end of the continent to the other. In their heyday the Indians were probably more widely travelled about the country than most early settlers of the Grand Traverse region, and certainly more knowledgeable about its geography.

The main Indian thoroughfare to the Grand Traverse region was the Saginaw-Mackinac Trail, which led from the mouth of the Detroit River to the Straits of Mackinac. Just north of Higgins Lake the Trail forked into two branches, one of which continued due north to the Straits and the other swung northwest across Kalkaska County and then north again to the narrows between Elk Lake and Skegemog Lake. From there it more or less followed the Lake Michigan shoreline up to Little Traverse Bay, Cross Village and the Straits.

There is good evidence that until recent times this trail has been in continuous use for as long as 10,000 years. That would make the Saginaw-Mackinac Trail at least twice as old as the pyramids at Giza. Carbon datings from an ancient campsite on the Trail indicate that it was first used by Paleo-Indian hunters pursuing the big game along the fringes of the retreating glacial ice sheet

some 8,000 years B.C. Known as the Samels Site, because it lies on a farm at Skegemog Point owned by the Samels brothers, the campsite was excavated and explored during several summers in the nineteen-sixties by a team of archeologists from Michigan State University. Among the multitude of Indian artifacts discovered there, was a beautifully fluted Folsom point, dating back from eight to ten thousand years. Many Folsom points have been found in southern Michigan but, until this discovery, none farther north than Clare County.

Another heavily travelled Indian trail led from East Grand Traverse Bay to Cadillac. It followed the line of hills east of Four Mile Road, then veered southeast along what is now the Supply Road, then due south around Indian Lake, crossing the Boardman River at Scheck's Campground. From there it angled southeast across the pine plains and south to Walton Junction, and crossed the Manistee River just east of the bridge on US-131.

Parts of this trail are clearly visible around Indian Lake, but Rennie Lake Road has obliterated much of it from there to the Boardman.

Another well-travelled trail led from Northport to Croton on the Muskegon River, a route followed by one of the earliest state roads to the Grand Traverse region. It was along this trail that Traverse City's first mail-carrier, Indian Jake Ta-pa-sah, brought the mail up from Croton in the early 1850s. Later, other Indians with dog sleds used the trail in winter to carry the mail from the south to Traverse City and the Straits. State road M-37 follows the old Indian trail pretty closely.

Another local trail ran from Boardman Lake down the west side of the Boardman River to Cadillac, crossing the Manistee River about half way between Baxter and Sherman. Still another ran to Manistee. Mail was carried over this route by way of Benzonia, first by Indians on foot or with dog teams, later by white men on horseback.

Wilderness Roads

It seems almost incredible that in 1862, eleven years after the establishment of the Traverse City settlement by Perry Hannah and the Hannah, Lay Company, there wasn't a single road leading to the Grand Traverse region, not one. The village, of course, was still very small, with a population of only about 300 inhabitants, and the entire region —comprising the counties of Grand Traverse, Antrim, Leelanau-Benzie and Kalkaska — contained fewer than 4,000 people of whom four or five hundred were Indians.

An article in the *Grand Traverse Herald* on February 21, 1862, describes the village as follows:

Traverse City, at the head of the West Bay, is the County seat . . . It has one double gang saw mill, which turns out 12,000,000 feet per annum; a Steam Flooring Mill, two Stores, two Hotels, one Printing office, one School-house, three Shoe Shops, one Blacksmith Shop, one Carpenter and Joiner's Shop, one Physician, one Lawyer, and no whiskey shop. The United States Land Office for the Traverse City District is located here.

The site commands the Bay and its charming scenery for twenty miles, while in the rear of the town, and partly embraced within its limits, we have the beautiful Boardman Lake, with its sloping banks, which covers three or four hundred acres, and through which the Boardman River flows and empties into the Bay at this point. This lake is of unknown depth, clear as crystal, and filled with trout, pickerel, pike, bass, perch, and many other varieties of fish.

The article goes on to describe Grand Traverse County:

The Township of Traverse embraces all that part of the county lying south of the Bay, being twelve six-mile-square townships. The county is settled (sparsely) for twelve or fourteen miles south of Traverse City, and for four or five miles east. In the neighborhood of Silver Lake (six miles south of the Bay) there is a considerable settlement of farmers, and the land in that immediate vicinity is nearly all taken up, but still farther south, and on the line of both of the State Roads, choice farming lands are open to all actual settlers for fifty cents an acre. The timber is principally maple and beech. And the soil is a rich sandy loam.

In every direction the country is well watered with small clear lakes, running brooks and springs, and there are no stagnant pools or marshes to cause ague or bilious fever.

(The two State Roads referred to had been surveyed and brushed out but were not yet under construction.)

Of local roads between settlements in the region there were only three. One ran from Traverse City up the Peninsula to Old Mission, on the same line as the Center Road follows today; it had been established around 1858. Another, which followed the curve of East Bay to Acme, was built about the same time. The third ran south for eight or ten miles to what is now Monroe Center. There was no road to the west of the village except one that followed the shore of West Bay from Traverse City to Greilick's or Norristown, (now called Greilickville).

The road south around Silver Lake to Monroe Center had been originally hacked out of the wilderness by the first settler of Grand Traverse County south of Traverse City, Lyman Smith. He brought his family by boat to Traverse City in 1853 and settled on Silver Lake. It took them two days to cut a trail over the eight miles to their homestead. It was said that Smith later got into the cattle business and brought many herds in over the Indian trail from Grand Rapids, travelling that route twenty-three times before the State Road was opened up. William Monroe and his family were the Smith's first neighbors. They came by sailboat to Traverse City in 1859. The village of Monroe Center was named after him.

Although there were no roads to the Traverse region in 1862, ten years later there were good roads throughout the region, north and south, east and west.

The eighteen-sixties were a time of great road-building activity in Michigan. By an act of Congress, the state had been granted thousands of acres of Federally owned swamp lands with the provision that the receipts from the sale of this land be used to drain and reclaim the swamps. But instead of spending the money for this purpose, the state decided to use it for building roads — quite rightly believing that new settlers along the highways would take it upon themselves to reclaim the swamps on their lands. (Compare this attitude toward swamps with the general conviction today that all remaining wetlands should be carefully preserved.)

Thus, with little expense to the people, roads were laid out all through the Grand Traverse region during the 1860s. The four principal roads were from Traverse City to Little Traverse Bay by way of Elk Rapids and Charlevoix; from Northport to Newaygo; from Traverse City to Manistee by way of Benzonia; and from Midland City to Traverse City by way of Houghton Lake. Another state road, begun in 1872, ran from East Grand Traverse Bay at Acme, through Grayling, to Harrisville on Lake Huron.

The roads of course were not built continuously in line but in segments often widely separated in time and space. The 30-mile segment of the Northport-Newaygo road from Traverse City to Northport, for example, was begun in 1862 and it was finished several years before the entire road was completed.

Deacon Joseph Dame, one of the pioneers at Northport, was one of the first to travel the barely passable road. He described the journey in the columns of the *Grand Traverse Herald* on March 1, 1862.

The old Settlers and Pioneers, learning that the State Road was cut out and made passable to Traverse City, a distance of about thirty miles, the Old Deacon, a man nearly 70 years of age, took his cane and started on foot and alone to examine the route and country through the wilderness, and the first day he travelled thirteen miles, to the last house before entering the wilderness. The next day he went through to the City.

The Deacon was followed next day by a team of horses and wagon carrying his wife,

Captain Nelson, and William Voice and his wife. Their journey is also described by the Old Deacon:

Left Northport Feb. 28th, at six o'clock a.m.; came on without any accident to a Public House about 17 miles from Northport, and stopped for dinner and to bait [feed] the team. A description of the Hotel and its accommodations are thus described: The house is about ten feet square — built of small logs and poles; it is about four feet high; had to enter on all fours; and in the other end of the house there was a place to build a fire with a hole left in the roof (which was covered with basswood bark) for the smoke to go out; and there were two beds on each side, made of hemlock branches. After building a fire, the company partook of a good dinner of cold ham, cold boiled beef, cake and cheese, etc. There being a beautiful stream of pure spring water running near the house, it afforded plenty of the best of Adam's ale for man and beast. After a little rest and refreshment the company gave their names and left; and as there was no landlord to collect the bills, they are still unpaid.

Construction of the new state roads was done mostly by local contractors who hired local farmers and others with teams of horses. Almost without exception the early state roads followed the route of the Indian trails. The roadway was generally one hundred feet wide. It was first cleared of timber and grubbed out for a distance of forty feet on either side of the center line. An additional ten feet on each side was "low chopped" to receive the rubbish from the center. The roadbed was then plowed so as to level the surface and remove all big stones and roots.

After the roadbed had been thus prepared, parallel ditches were dug on each side, leaving about sixty feet between them. The ditches were about three feet deep, eleven feet wide at the top and two at the bottom. In ordinary dry grounds, the earth from the ditches was used to raise the level of the road, which was crowned slightly to provide good drainage. The finished road was about thirty feet wide, with a hard, smooth, graded surface of sand and gravel. Bridges were about twenty feet wide and built of squared

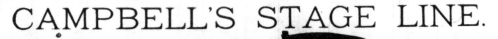

CAMPBELL'S STAGE LINE.

Campbell's Stage Office, }
Traverse City, January 1, 1872. }

TO THOSE THUSLY CONCERNED:

I notice an article in the Traverse Bay Eagle, No. 38, taken from the Big Rapids Independent, relative to stageing between Clam Lake and Traverse City. Come on, brother Hutchinson, you are welcomed in this enterprise. There's lots of room up here,

Among the treezes
And northern breezes.

Our people will be glad to see you, with a heap of money to scatter along said proposed route through the unbroken wilderness, and in the darkness of night your drivers will be charmed with the music of hooting owls and howling wolves.

TO MY PATRONS AND FRIENDS:

You have my sincere thanks for past favors, and with reasonable rates and honorable dealings, (Motto, "SECOND TO NONE,") I hope to receive in the future a share of public patronage.

"THE WORLD MOVES," and I don't care a fig if everybody knows that

CAMPBELL'S U. S. MAIL STAGES

Make connections between TRAVERSE CITY, via. SHERMAN, to RAILROAD, at

CLAM LAKE, EVERY DAY EACH WAY,

In Sunshine or Shower, and through the settled and flourishing farming country in Grand Traverse and Wexford Counties, and connecting at Traverse City with the only line of

United States Mail and Express Stages

For Elk Rapids, Clarlevoix, Little Traverse and Cheboygan, Glen Arbor, Old Mission, Northport, Leland, Benzonia, Frankfort and Manistee. With my new outfit in BUFFALO ROBES, LAP ROBES, FOOT PANS, ETC.,found in every sleigh, experienced, kind, sober and obliging drivers, that have been in my employ for eighteen months, is evidence sufficient that they "are of the right stamp." I am prepared to offer inducements to the

TRAVELING PUBLIC

Never before found in this northern country; connecting with the cars to the Outside World in ONE DAY. I have also a largely increased force of Men, Horses and Sleighs to do ANY and ALL business in Passengers, Express or Freight that may be entrusted to my care with promptness and dispatch, between Traverse City and Railroad at Clam Lake and Big Rapids, and through the entire Northwestern Michigan. My

LINE OF STAGES,

Passing through the Counties of Grand Traverse, Leelanau, Benzie, Manistee, Wexford, Lake, Newaygo, Mecosta, Antrim, Charlevoix and Emmet.

Also a complete suit of Extra Rigs kept at Traverse City and Clam Lake to carry Passengers at all times, and to any part of the country, far or near, with Terms, Speed, etc., to suit the times.

With my past experience and present facilities for filling orders and delivering Passengers, Express or Freight entrusted to my care, I challenge competition.

Mark Freight to Care Campbell's Stage Line.

H. D. CAMPBELL, Prop'r.

HERALD SUPPLEMENT.

Grand Traverse Herald, January 1, 1872.

timbers, as were the embankments on both sides of the waterway. In country where the ground was low and marshy, the roadbed was built up to a height of at least three feet above the standing water; the base of these causeways was first covered with fascines — slender poles and branches tied up in bundles thirty feet in length and seven to nine inches in diameter. They were fastened down with long wooden pins, and the dirt from the ditches was thrown on top. Culverts were also built of heavy squared timbers.

The first to be completed to the Traverse area was the road from Newaygo to Northport, a distance of about 140 miles. Long before it was completely finished around 1867, it was open for horses and wagons. Travellers had to be ferried across the Manistee River at Sherman on a horsedrawn raft guided by a rope cable stretched between the riverbanks.

The completion of the first state roads to the area in the late sixties and early seventies, the Homestead Act of 1863, the coming of the first railroad in 1872, and the opening up of the Indian reserves to homesteaders in 1874 — all these combined to bring about a great influx of new settlers to the Grand Traverse region during the 1870s.

Stagecoaches

Although stagecoach lines were in operation in southern Michigan by the early 1800s, they did not reach the Grand Traverse region until the late 1860s. The reason for that is obvious: there were no suitable roads in the area until that time. Nevertheless, as early as 1865, James K. Gunton, proprietor of the Gunton House on Traverse City's East Front street, ran a coach line to Muskegon during the winter months when the sleighing was good. Although the road to Muskegon was still impassable to all wheel vehicles except wagons, a covered coach on runners, drawn by a team of horses, could — and did —make the 150-mile journey over the snow in four days. Gunton's Line left the Gunton House at seven o'clock every Monday morning, and left Muskegon on the return trip at seven a.m. on Saturday. There were intermediate stops at Benzonia, Bear Lake, Norwalk, Manistee, Freesoil, Lincoln, Pere Marquette (Ludington), Pentwater and White Lake.

The following year, three stagecoach companies announced their winter schedule for 1866-'67:

While the Sleighing is Good
Line of Stages will Run from Traverse City to Muskegon in 3 days.

Leaving Traverse City every Monday, Wednesday and Friday at 7 a.m.

Return leaving Muskegon every Tuesday, Thursday and Saturday at 7 a.m., stopping both ways for the night at Manistee and Pentwater.

And to take on and leave off passengers or freight at White Lake, Pere Marquette, Lincoln, Freesoil, Norwalk, Pleasanton, Benzonia, Homestead, Sherman's or any other point on the route.

Express goods carried with safety and responsibility. Accommodations good, fares low and quicker time than any other line.

> Steward & Baily
> Rody & Collins
> Pettinger & Co.

It was not until 1870 that Traverse City and the region got its first regular year-around stagecoach service. In the spring of that year, Henry D. Campbell initiated the first "express mail" stagecoach line between Traverse City and Big Rapids. Campbell was one of Traverse City's earliest pioneers. He came to Traverse City in 1852 and worked a few years for the Hannah, Lay Company, then got married and did some farming. In 1861, after the election of Abraham Lincoln, he became Traverse City's second postmaster, replacing Dr. D. C. Goodale, whose assistant he had been since 1853. Although Campbell held the office for only a year, he continued to serve as supervisor of mails for the Grand Traverse region.

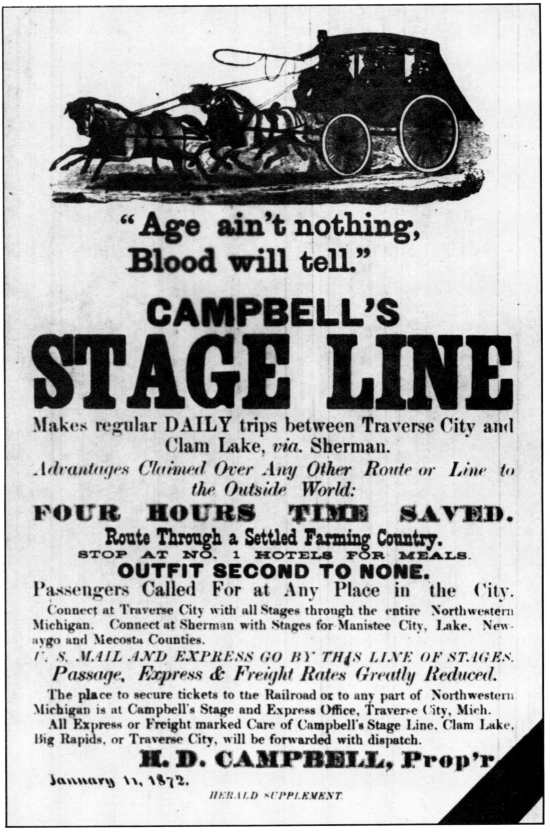

Grand Traverse Herald, January 11, 1872.

By 1870, the Grand Rapids & Indiana Railroad, in its progress north from Grand Rapids, had reached Big Rapids; and in May of that year Henry Campbell opened stagecoach service to connect with the railroad at that place, carrying mail, express freight and passengers.

You had to get up early to catch Campbell's stagecoach express. It left at five o'clock in the morning—one of Campbell's advertising slogans was "The Early Bird Catches the Worm". The trip took two days and the fare was $6. Passengers were assured of "a Square Meal at 6:30 every morning", at a tavern eight miles south of Traverse City.

Late in the following year, when the railroad reached Cadillac (or Clam Lake, as it was called then), Campbell offered one-day service to connect with the railroad at that place, for $4, while continuing to run his line to Big Rapids. With the initiation of connecting stagecoach service to the Grand Rapids & Indiana at Clam Lake, the *Grand Traverse Herald* commented: "The days of the long stage line to get outside are gone forever."

About that same time Campbell got some competition from a man named Hutchinson of Big Rapids, who opened a rival line from Big Rapids to Clam Lake and Fife Lake. Campbell doesn't seem to have worried much about it. In a big ad in the Herald on January 4, 1872, he welcomes "brother Hutchinson" and challenges him to the rivalry; this ad, and others he ran at the time, make interesting and amusing reading.

Campbell was a man of great energy, intelligence and wit, and he had a long and distinguished career in Traverse City. By 1872 his stage lines were operating all over northern Michigan: south to Big Rapids, with connections at Sherman for Clam Lake and Lake City; north to Elk Rapids, Charlevoix, Little Traverse and Cheboygan; west to Benzonia, Frankfort and Manistee; locally to Glen Arbor, Leland, Northport and Old Mission.

In 1871 Campbell bought two lots on the corner of Park and State Street from Victor Petertyl, and in 1873 built the Campbell House, later known as the Park Place Hotel. He remained sole owner and proprietor until 1878, when the hotel was leased by (and later sold to) the Hannah, Lay Company. Campbell gave up the stagecoach lines in 1874 and turned them over to his younger brother, Robert A. Campbell, who operated them, on a slowly diminishing scale, until some time in the 1880s. Henry Campbell went on to build the first Traverse City public water works in 1881, and in 1890 the first electric light plant. He also served for twelve years as a probate judge.

The stagecoaches used by Campbell and others in Michigan were of the familiar "mail express" Concord type, which was developed simultaneously in the 1830s at Concord, New Hampshire, and Troy, New York. They had sleek, swell-sided bodies which were suspended between front and rear axles on leather thoroughbraces. There was a luggage rail on the flat top, and a luggage boot behind. The driver sat high up in front.

Inside, the passengers sat on transverse rows of seats facing each other, and the coaches could carry from 6 to 16 passengers; additional passengers could be accommodated on the driver's seat and sometimes on the top in good weather.

Mail coaches were drawn by four horses, the slower coaches by two. The speed was between four and ten miles an hour, depending on the condition of the road, and there were frequent stops to rest the horses. The mail coach driver was king of the road — everything in its path had to get out of the way. As the stage neared a tavern, postoffice or lodging house, the driver sounded his approach by blowing on a long tin horn which was carried in a sheath at his side.

Few people living today in Michigan ever rode a stagecoach. But there are some excellent accounts written at the time by

RAILROADS!

TELEGRAPH,
NAVIGATION CLOSED,
WINTRY WEATHER
STAGING,
And How's Your Epizootic To-Day?
Going Outside!

All have their places. "Time and tide wait for no man." Midst all the changes, tumult, excitement and hum of biz,

CAMPBELL'S
MAIL & EXPRESS STAGES

Continue to run as heretofore over 3300 miles weekly, deliver and receive the U. S. Mails at post offices 420 times every week—supplying thousands of the reading public in the Counties of Grand Traverse, Wexford, Benzie, Leelanau, Manistee, Lake, Newaygo, Mecosta, Kalkaska, Missaukee, Antrim, Charlevoix and Emmet, with the news of the day; carrying hundreds of travelers on their way comfortably, and handling tons of Express with safety and dispatch.

Inquire at Campbell's Stage and Express office, Traverse City, or of my Agent on the Traverse City Express train between Traverse City and Clam Lake, for information touching facilities of travel or dispatching Express north from Traverse City, Mich.

MAIL & EXPRESS STAGES LEAVE AS FOLLOWS:

Leave Traverse City every Monday, Wednesday and Friday, at 7 a. m., for Elk Rapids, Brownstown, Charlevoix and the only direct mail connection to Little Traverse, Cheboygan, Mackinac and the Upper Peninsula.

Extras will leave my stables Monday, Wednesday and Friday evening after Express train arrives via Elk Rapids, connecting with regular mail stages at Brownstown for the north the following morning (on demand.) By this arrangement passengers leaving Grand Rapids at 10 a. m. arrive at Elk Rapids the same day and Charlevoix 12 m. next day.

Also for Elk Rapids every Tuesday, Thursday and Saturday at 7 a. m., returning the same day, forming the best possible connections from Traverse City north.

Leave Traverse City Monday and Thursday, 7 a. m., connecting at Glen Arbor with mail stages for Glen Haven, Frankfort and Leland, returning the next day.

Leave Traverse City, 7 a. m., every morning for Monroe Center, Wexford, connecting at Sherman with Wheatland, Clay Hill, Manton and Manistee stages, returning every day.

Leave Traverse City Wednesday and Saturday at 7 a. m. for Old Mission, returning the same day.

[Leave Traverse City Tuesday and Friday for Benzonia, Frankfort and Manistee, and for Northport Monday, Wednesday and Friday, returning the following day. Prop., T. A. H.]

P. S.—*Remember that my CALL BUSS will run to trains regular, and will answer all calls for Passengers, Baggage, Express and freight, to and from trains, hotels and private houses.*

Inquire at Campbell's Stage & Express Office, Traverse City, Mich., for any information for lost Baggage, Express or Freight, or Railroad Tickets anywhere in the United States or Canadas.

JANUARY, 1873.

H. D. CAMPBELL, Prop.

Grand Traverse Herald, January 18, 1873.

people who did, including the following by George B. Catlin in *Michigan History*, 1948:

Horses were frequently changed and at each place of change there was a wayside inn with both solid and liquid refreshments and a huge watering trough. The ladies would get out to shake their skirts and stretch their "limbs" (there were no legs in stagecoach days). The men would enter the barroom "to see a man" and emerge with suspicious breaths but looking refreshed, and the stage would dash away with the cracking of the driver's whip and sometimes the tootling of a bugle.

The stagecoach in the Grand Traverse region had a fairly short life. By the 1890s there were five railroads in the area, and they soon made the stagecoach obsolete.

CAMPBELL HOUSE,
Traverse City, Mich.   H. D. Campbell, Prop.

"The Early Bird Catches the Worm."

CAMPBELL'S
MAIL STAGES

Go Loaded Every Day, with Whole Souled, Jolly, Good Feeling Passengers.

No Dead Beats go by this line of Stages ; Everybody is satisfied to pay the low fare of $4.00 to Railroad.

NO ADVANCE ON FARE WHEN OTHER LINES FAIL TO CONNECT.

No Complimentary Tickets Out over this Line.

No Bribing Landlords to keep Passengers for this Line

No Feeing the Printer for Spicy Locals or Colored Editorials.

Campbell Blows His Own Horn.

REMEMBER
This Line of Stages leaves Traverse City Every Morning at 5 o'clock.

REMEMBER
That passengers get a Square Meal at 6:30 every morning, eight miles from the city.

REMEMBER
This Line never fails to connect with the Cars at Clam Lake.

REMEMBER
This is the only Line of U. S. Mail and Express Stages passing through every County in Northwestern Michigan.

REMEMBER
This Line is second to none in Outfit, Speed, Rates of Fare for Passengers or Freight.

REMEMBER
This is the Cheapest Line.

REMEMBER
To secure your Tickets at Campbell's Stage and Express Office at Traverse City or Clam Take.

HERALD SUPPLEMENT.

Grand Traverse Herald, November 20, 1873.

93

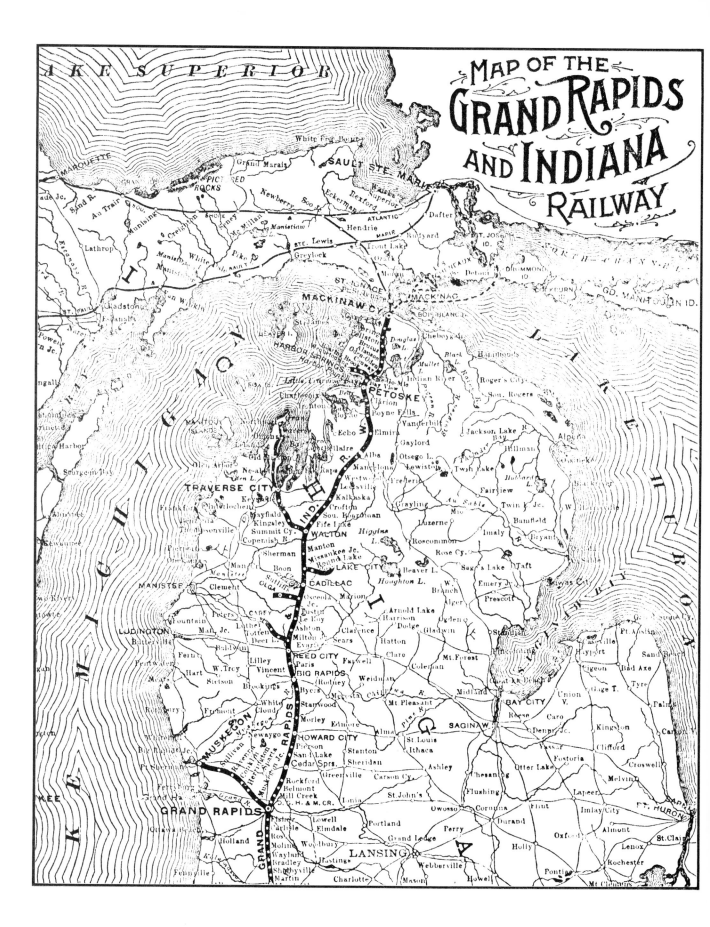

MAP OF THE GRAND RAPIDS AND INDIANA RAILWAY

94

Railroads

Grand Traverse Herald, September 4, 1893.

The Coming Of The Railroad

Grand Rapids & Indiana Railroad

When the first railroad train steamed into town on the evening of November 15, 1872, the people of Traverse City felt they were out of the woods at last. Up until that time their only contact with the outside world had been by sailing ship or steamer — and, during the four or five months when winter closed down navigation on the Great Lakes, only by tenuous stagecoach line. Now they could board a train and be in Detroit or Chicago within a few hours.

The coming of the railroad changed their lives, changed their thinking in ways subtle and profound. It wrought a change as revolutionary as the automobile was to do fifty years later. Until the railroad came, Traverse City people used the expression "going outside" when they spoke of a trip to Detroit or Chicago, or even Muskegon. "Perry Hannah made a trip outside last week," the *Grand Traverse Herald* would report, as if the Traverse region were some kind of Conradian "Heart of Darkness." After the railroad came, nobody used that expression any more. The railroad had brought the outside world to Traverse City.

The Grand Rapids & Indiana was one of the last of the land grant railroads. In 1856 Congress passed an act making grants of millions of acres of public land to several southern and midwestern states to encourage railroad building. The states in turn awarded land grants to private companies

95

formed for that purpose. Each recipient was required to build a railroad between two designated points within a specified length of time. There were other requirements and stipulations that in the long run made the grants less desirable than at first they appeared, but that is another story.

In 1857 the Grand Rapids & Indiana Railway Company was awarded a grant of 823,204 acres to build a railroad between Grand Rapids and some point on Traverse Bay. The Panic of 1857 and the Civil War held up construction until 1869, when the GR&I, after heroic efforts to raise the necessary capital, began to build its road into the wilderness north of Grand Rapids.

After that, the work went forward speedily. Cadillac was reached in 1871 and Petoskey in 1872; in 1874 the line was extended to the Straits of Mackinac. Meanwhile, in 1870, the road was completed from Ft. Wayne to Grand Rapids. The actual construction was done under contract by the Continental Improvement Company, a firm controlled by the Pennsylvania Railroad. Under the terms of the contract the GR&I had to hand over to that company its entire land grant, plus some $8,000,000 in bonds to be secured by the completed railroad.

Traverse City people had been unhappily aware since 1871 that the railroad was going to pass them by, and were determined to do something about it. In the spring of that year Perry Hannah was able to persuade General George W. Cass, President of the Continental Improvement Co., that a branch line to Traverse City was a viable project. Under the terms of the agreement Traverse City would put up $40,000 against a projected construction cost of some $260,000.

A survey of the proposed route was made that fall by Col. J. O. Hudnutt, Civil Engineer of the GR&I. It was begun on August 8 and finished on September 15. The Colonel reported an easy and favorable route. The junction with the GR&I would be made on the northeast corner of Section 33, Township 25 North, Range 10 West.

From that point west, the land was quite level for several miles. No difficulty would be encountered until the route dipped into the Boardman River valley just south of the Neal, Gibbs & Co. sawmill at Mayfield, where the route was rolling for several miles. The northern 8 miles into Traverse City was level. The length of the branch was just under 26 miles.

An association known as the Traverse City Rail Road Company formed in October of 1871. Its directors were Perry Hannah, Morgan Bates, E. W. Hulburd, Smith Barnes, J. D. Harvey, D. C. Leach and General Cass. Perry Hannah was elected president; Thomas T. Bates, secretary; and Charles A. Crawford, treasurer. After some difficulty the $40,000 was raised among the directors and by popular subscription, Hannah himself contributing $20,000. On January 11, 1872, the company signed a contract with Continental Improvement, and work on the new railroad was begun that spring. (The finished railroad was operated under lease by the Grand Rapids & Indiana until 1918, when the Traverse City Rail Road Company was finally dissolved.)

The company also made a contract with Hannah, Lay & Co. for the depot grounds. Under its terms the railroad would have the strip of land lying between the Boardman River and the Bay, beginning with the so-called "Point" at the mouth of the river and extending west to the foot of Park Street. This comprised about 9 acres of land with water frontage of more than 2300 feet. The railroad also received an additional 10 acres to the east of the Point to use in any way it saw fit. (Among other uses, a watertank and windmill were erected here.)

The contract for clearing, grubbing and grading was let to the firm of H. O. Rose of Northport and W. W. Barton of Leland. The right of way was to be cleared of timber and all stumps grubbed out to a distance of 100 feet on each side of the railroad bed. Rose & Barton hired a crew of 100 men at wages of $2 per day and began work as soon as the frost was out of the ground. After the trees were cut down and the stumps removed, they leveled and smoothed the grade using horse-drawn scoops and scrapers.

On July 11 the barge *East Saginaw* brought in a steam locomotive and 10 flat cars, along with a load of rails; and on July 16 the Hannah, Lay steamer, *City of Traverse,* unloaded the running gear for the flatcars. Meanwhile, a railroad bridge was built at the mouth of the river, and a roundhouse and small depot at the foot of Park Street. To the south, around the last of August, the GR&I was preparing to cross the Manistee River near Manton.

The job of grading and laying the cross-ties was completed by the first of October, and on the 10th of that month the schooner *David Stewart* unloaded 993 tons of rails at the Hannah, Lay dock. The rails were 45-pound iron, of the Fish bar pattern (as compared with today's rails of more than 100 pounds per yard). Ross & Barton's crew, now increased to 250 men at $2.50 a day, began laying them from both ends of the line: more rails had been brought up by the GR&I to the southern end of the line. At the same time, gangs of men on handcars were raising telegraph poles and stringing wire.

A "first" of sorts was recorded when C. A. Denniston's general store at Mayfield had the first goods delivered by the railroad. The goods were brought in on the *City of Traverse* and delivered to Mayfield by the construction train on October 31. Under the headline, "First Goods by Railroad", Denniston ran an ad in the *Herald* for the sale of dry goods, groceries, clothing, hardware, school books, stationery and "everything you'd expect to find in a country general store".

The last spike was driven and the first train arrived in Traverse City on November 15, 1872, as previously noted.

On that day the editor of the *Herald* wrote a short, exuberant piece for the paper entitled "Out of the Wilderness!" Twelve years ago,

Old GR&I engine. PIONEER STUDY CENTER

he wrote, when he first came to Traverse City, he had travelled from Grand Haven to Benzonia on a sandy wagon road, and thence to this town by little more than a footpath. Now, at last, the railroad had brought civilization to the region.

In the same issue of the *Herald* Rose & Barton advertised: "Cheap for Cash: 14 horses, harnesses, wagons, wheelbarrows, ploughs, shovels, grub hoes, blankets, bed ticks and all kinds of camp equipage used in building the Railroad."

Trains carrying passengers and freight began to operate almost immediately, and in April of 1873 the railroad issued its first regular time schedule. Southbound, the "express" train left Traverse City at 8:30

a.m., arriving at Grand Rapids at 5 p.m. and Kalamazoo at 7 p.m. On the return trip, the train left Kalamazoo at 8 a.m. and reached Traverse City at 6 p.m.

In addition to the express, there was a local train to Clam Lake (Cadillac) which departed Traverse City at 2 in the afternoon and arrived there at 7:10. The train from Clam Lake left at 6:00 in the morning and reached Traverse City at 11:20.

The coming of the railroad marked the real opening up of the Grand Traverse region. Within a short time the railroad brought in more new settlers and worldly goods than had ever been carried by the sailing ships and steamers. And the railroad gave Traverse City mills and small factories ready access to

GR&I Depot, 1897. EDWARD BARDY COLLECTION

GR&I train, 1893.
MICHIGAN STATE UNIVERSITY HISTORICAL ARCHIVES

urban markets unavailable by water. Among the many products shipped by rail from the Grand Traverse area during the next sixty years were thousands of carloads of all kinds of forest products including lumber, hardwood flooring, plywood and charcoal; baskets, furniture and pig iron; cherries and potatoes, apples and pears and peaches and pickles; motor trucks and malleable castings; and, believe it or not, before artificial refrigeration was invented, as many as 20 carloads of ice each day in the summer to southern Michigan, Ohio and Indiana.

Like all other Michigan railroads, the GR&I reached its peak in the early decades of the 20th century, then began to go downhill. Passenger service burgeoned as freight loadings fell off. The great "resort specials" brought in thousands of summer visitors each year — the GR&I ran as many as six passenger trains daily into the Grand Traverse region during the summer — and the railroads were actively engaged in promoting the tourist industry. But, as all railroads had to find out sooner or later —you can't run a railroad on passengers alone.

In 1903 the GR&I made an attempt to boost its declining revenues by establishing a cross-lake car ferry service to Manistique. The Traverse City, Leelanau and Manistique railroad from Traverse City to Northport was built for that purpose, but the project was ultimately a failure. In 1921 the Pennsylvania railroad, which had controlling interest in the GR&I from the beginning, took over the ailing line and began to operate it under a 999-year lease. The GR&I had never shown much of a profit after the timber was gone, but it still served as an important feeder line for the Pennsylvania system.

Few American railroads died a sudden death: like the old soldiers of legend they just seemed to fade away. Or like the Cheshire cat, the disappearing process was slow: one year the smile at least was there, next year you looked around and it was gone. The Pennsylvania drastically cut back its passenger service in the late thirties, and by 1948 it was running only one train in and out of Traverse City each day — and only during the summer months. In 1949 it discontinued all passenger service north of Cadillac.

Shortly after the end of World War II the Pennsy built a new railroad yard and a small depot in Traverse City just south of 8th Street on Woodmere. The old passenger station, freight warehouse and tracks were removed from the City waterfront in 1949 to make way for the new Grandview Parkway and the development of Clinch Park. (The railroad leased its waterfront property to the City for one dollar a year.)

In 1973 the Pennsylvania got permission from the Interstate Commerce Commission to abandon its 246 miles of broken-down track from Grand Rapids to the Straits of Mackinac. This left Traverse City with only one railroad outlet, the Chesapeake & Ohio.

Then, in 1976, the trackage was leased by a small group of railroad buffs, who had lots of love for railroads but little or no experience with running them. They included four young men and a 31-year-old mother, Elizabeth Andrus, who became president of the company. Together they formed the Michigan Northern Railroad, with headquarters at Cadillac, and began to operate a freight line on government subsidy. Despite frequent derailments and other mishaps (the track is so bad in places that the engineer must reduce his speed to five miles an hour or less), the line continues in operation today — but not to Traverse City. After an inspection by the state Department of Transportation in the fall of 1979, the 26-mile branch from Walton was declared unsafe and closed down. Up to that time Michigan Northern had been serving only five customers in Traverse City and running just one car per week on the line.

The GR&I had its share of wrecks and mishaps over the years. Those are the things that people remember, but it should be pointed out that its safety record, like that of most railroads in those days, was remarkably good.

One of the most amusing accidents happened in the summer of 1890. A Reed City

Grand Rapids & Indiana Railway.

TRAIN SERVICE, SEASON 1903.

The train service to Northern Michigan for the season 1903 will be improved, and will go into effect on Sunday, June 21st, and continue until September 26th, inclusive.

THE NORTHLAND LIMITED

formerly known as the Northland Express, will be strictly a *limited train* and will run on about its former schedule, leaving Cincinnati, Pennsylvania Station, at 7:00 P. M. daily, with through sleeping cars to Petoskey and Mackinaw City, and also to Traverse City and Northport, arriving at those points the next forenoon.

Sleeping car will leave Louisville via the Penna. Lines at about 3:30 P. M. daily, Indianapolis about 6:45 P. M., and St. Louis via the Vandalia Line, about 12:30 Noon, running via Richmond, and will be attached to the "Northland Limited" at that point.

Dining cars will be run on these trains between St. Louis, Louisville and Richmond.

Sleeping car will leave Chicago daily via the Michigan Central R. R. at about 10:00 P. M., and will be attached to this train at Kalamazoo.

Dining car will be attached at Grand Rapids, serving meals a la carte.

The new road from TRAVERSE CITY to NORTHPORT will be opened for traffic about July 1st, when through sleepers will be run from Cincinnati to Northport, thus accommodating passengers desiring to visit Northport, Omena and other Grand Traverse Bay Resorts.

Connections will also be made at Traverse City with the Traverse Bay Line Steamers as formerly.

man named Belknapp was returning home late at night on the GR&I after a business trip to the north. Hearing the brakeman call out, "Reed City", he picked up his valise and went to the door. When the train came to a stop he descended the steps in the dark and, grip in hand, plunged 12 feet into the Hersey River. The train had stopped to take on water just north of the town, leaving the cars on the bridge over the river. He fished himself out of the river unhurt, suffering only the loss of his baggage and his dignity, but a newspaper story next day called him the angriest passenger on the Grand Rapids & Indiana.

Another mishap that could have been serious but wasn't, took place on a Saturday afternoon, January 14, 1903. Between 4:30 and 5:00 the way freight was switching cars in the yard at Kingsley when the brake on one of the boxcars failed and it took off with a flying start down into the Boardman River valley. There was a brakeman named Dooley on the car and he did his best with the brake wheel but the car kept on picking up speed.

The GR&I railroad men had always held that the grade was so steep south of Kingsley to the river that a car getting loose at Kingsley would run all the way to Traverse City. What worried engineer Daily and conductor Phil Griffin was that the 4:30 passenger train had already left Traverse City, and there was no way in the world that anybody could get in touch with crew aboard.

Daily threw the six cars ahead of his engine onto a side track, swung the engine out on the main track and raced after the runaway car at full throttle. When the pursuing engine came into the straight stretch through Mayfield, the car was just going out of sight over a mile ahead, having gone through Mayfield like a rocket.

The engine overtook the car near the bridge across the Boardman between Mayfield and Sleights. Griffin made the coupling on the run, and a flagman was dropped off to run ahead and flag down the passenger train.

As it turned out, the train had stopped at Sleights to let off a number of passengers; otherwise, the train men said, they wouldn't have been able to recover the car in time to prevent a wreck. No harm done, engineer Daily backed up with the car to Kingsley, with the passenger train following close behind.

The theory about a runaway car running all the way to Traverse City if left to itself was proved correct forty-five years later. On September 8, 1948, two fully loaded coal cars got away from a side track at Kingsley and roared down through the Boardman valley. They demolished a railroad inspection car near Sleights (the sixteen men aboard jumped to safety with only seconds to spare), tore through Traverse City at 100 miles an hour, flew off the end of the track at the GR&I station near the waterfront, and landed in a municipal parking lot at Clinch Park, spewing coal all over the place.

Southbound GR&I passenger train derailed
1½ miles south of Westwood by broken rail.
Several injuries, no fatalities. Sept. 2, 1916.
TRAVERSE CITY RECORD-EAGLE

G R & I WRECK. WESTWOOD, MICH. SEP. 2-16

&I WRECK. WESTWOOD, MICH SEPT 2-16

Double Trouble on the Pennsy

Cock crow. Wednesday, September 8, 1948. Sunrise at 6:09. A clear brisk late-summer day. Chance of showers by late afternoon. Most of the summer visitors have departed. The kids are back in school. Things are getting back to normal.

At Kingsley, a village 18 miles south of Traverse City, Winnie Pierce, assistant track foreman — the "first man" in railroad lingo —opens up the Pennsylvania Railroad depot at seven o'clock. It's his job to gas up the "putt-putts", lay out the tools and check the train orders for the day. Entering the tool shed at one end of the depot, he notices that two fully loaded coal cars are standing on a siding a few hundred yards away.

Ten or fifteen minutes later, two men who work for Leslie Walton, the local coal distributor, drive up in a truck and prepare to set up the conveyor for loading trucks. First they must move the cars a few feet so that the unloading pockets in the floor of the cars are centered exactly over the elevator openings in the railroad bed. To do this they must move a weight of some 150 tons. But, no problem: with the use of a pinching bar (an iron bar, five feet long, with a jack-like "dog" and a flattened end) it's a lot easier than it sounds. One man climbs up on one of the cars to operate the hand-brake, the other starts pinching the cars forward.

But suddenly the cars begin to roll much faster than they should. The man on the car hollers that the brake won't hold. His partner drops the pinching bar, grabs a loose tie and shoves it under the wheels. The moving cars brush the cross-tie out of the way and roll on ahead, picking up speed. The man at the brake waits as long as he dares, tugging at the wheel, then jumps for his life.

It all happens in a matter of seconds. The two men watch helplessly as the cars roll away, career through a switch and go out of sight around a curve. From Kingsley to Mayfield the grade is very steep, and the cars will pick up tremendous speed as they barrel down into the Boardman River valley.

Meanwhile, Lyle "Hap" Sheridan, whose back yard lies on the coal siding, hears the sound of the moving cars, glances out of his kitchen window and sees the cars roll away, out of control. He runs outside and talks with the two Walton men, who tell him what has happened.

Sheridan is a mason who works for a construction firm in Traverse City. He's ready to leave for work, and so jumps into his car and heads north on County Road 611, thinking he may be able to warn people along the way.

After some indecision one of the two Walton men runs up the track to the depot. Here he finds Winnie Pierce in the tool shed and explains what has happened. Pierce telephones Leo McGee, the agent at Traverse City, and tells him. So far, so good.

Pierce is more annoyed than apprehensive. He assumes—as do all the others—that the cars will come to a stop somewhere in the Boardman River valley. Probably that will happen south of Keystone Dam, where the cars must climb a long grade. He is annoyed at the two Walton men because, under strict railroad rules, they should not have moved the cars; they should have waited for a section crew to do the job. Nevertheless, no great harm done — or so he thinks.

But, back at the Traverse City depot, agent McGee is very worried. Aside from the good chance of someone getting hurt at one of the many road crossings between Kingsley and Keystone, there is a major problem. At 7:30 this morning — just a few minutes ago — 14 railroad officials from Philadelphia and Chicago have taken off on the rails in an inspection car to check the track and bridges between Traverse City and Cadillac. Where is that car now? Will the men in the vehicle see the runaway cars in time to get off the track? Will they all be killed?

McGee figures there's a chance that the officials may have stopped on the south side of town, where local crews are building a new switchyard. He jumps in his car and heads across town for the yard. There he finds that the section foreman, Verl McManus, has just left to check out something at the depot: their paths must have crossed. McGee talks with Vernol Stauffer, the assistant foreman. He learns that the inspection car with its 14 passengers has passed by without stopping ten minutes ago. (Recalling it today, Stauffer says with a grin, "I remember thinking that we all ought to come to attention and salute as those Pennsy big-wigs went by.")

After talking with Stauffer, McGee heads back to the depot. There he meets McManus, and the two men discuss what can be done. McGee has already notified the police.

They decide that — except to pray for the safety of the men on the inspection car — nothing much can be done now. But just to do *something*, and to play it safe (though neither man believes the coal cars will get this far), McGee walks down the tracks from the depot and throws a switch that will route traffic to the house-track, a dead end siding.

Meanwhile, back at the switchyard, Stauffer jumps in his car and heads across town to find his boss, Verl McManus. At a nearby street crossing he pulls up behind a big milk tank-truck. He hears somebody holler, "Watch out! Watch out!" and looks around. He sees the two coal cars coming down the track like a bat out of hell.

"They were bouncing up and down on their springs, raising a cloud of dust," Vernol recalls. "I knew they must be going at least a hundred miles an hour. They hit those iron gates at the C&O crossing, and the gates just disappeared. One fellow says he saw part of one gate sailing up the hill two blocks away. They never did find all those pieces." (The Chesapeake & Ohio railroad crosses the Pennsylvania just north of the southside switchyard.) "They sure took the dust off that milk truck," Vernol adds.

"One of the trackmen at the switchyard ran over and put a little piece of board on the rail just before the coal cars came roaring through," Vernol goes on. "Just a little piece of board." He laughs. "Well, he tried."

Back at the depot, Verl McManus on the depot platform hears them coming.

"McGee had just thrown the switch and was coming back when we heard them," McManus says. "There was a great roar, like a tornado. How they made it around the curve just before the river and across the trestle I'll never know. That trestle wasn't strong. It had a speed limit of only ten miles an hour. But those cars were going so fast that the bridge never had time to collapse."

At the end of the house-track there was only a bunting block — capable of stopping a car going two or three miles an hour. The coal cars demolished it.

"I stood there and watched it," Verl McManus says. "Those cars sailed through the air like a couple of big birds. They smashed into the parking lot at the end of the track and spewed coal all over it. One car came down piggy-back on the other. It was lucky there were no automobiles in the lot." (The parking lot was below the level of the dead-end track.)

It was now ten minutes of eight. The wild ride of the coal cars from Kingsley to Traverse City had taken about twenty minutes.

Now the trainmen really begin to worry. What has happened to those sixteen men? Where are they? Were they able to get off the track in time?

"We began to have gruesome thoughts," says Vernol Stauffer. "Plenty of times I helped shovel up cattle and sheep hit by the train. I was really worried. I didn't know what we were going to find out there."

After the runaway cars came past the switchyard, Vernol Stauffer and several other trainmen jumped in their cars and raced south along the road that follows the railroad tracks through the Boardman River valley. They didn't have far to go.

Just before reaching a big curve half a mile north of the river, the tracks run straight for about a mile. It was on this stretch of track that the driver of the inspection truck saw the coal cars come flying down the rails.

The inspection vehicle looked something like an army personnel carrier. It had a canvass top, and, inside, two parallel rows of seats along each side. The back end was open. The passengers could see out behind but not ahead. Only the men in the driver's seat forward could see down the track ahead.

The driver, thinking there's been a mix-up in train orders, brakes the truck to a stop. He and his partner jump out to flag down the train. But then they realize it isn't a train at all.

Shouting, "Jump! Jump!", they run back and help the officials scramble out of the truck. All make the leap to safety — all except one elderly man who is poised to jump when the impact occurs. They watch him sail through the air in a dreadful kind of slow motion, his long white hair streaming out behind. Miraculously, he is thrown clear and gets to his feet slowly but unhurt.

The truck is a total wreck. It is lifted in the air and comes down athwart the rails. The coal cars, without even a pause, continue on their wild ride.

The collision occured at Mackey Crossing, a private road near Sleight's siding (where years ago there was a sawmill and potato warehouse). People living nearby heard the crash and came running. The officials were loaded into three autos and driven to Traverse City. They met the cars of the trackmen about half a mile south of the switchyard.

"It was a miracle," says Vernol Stauffer. "A miracle that noboby got hurt or even scratched. Those cars had to pass forty road crossings between Kingsley and the depot at Traverse City.

"And it was a miracle that saved those Pennsy officials," he goes on. "You know, that was the only straight stretch of track in the whole Boardman valley. If they'd been a quarter mile farther along, or a quarter mile back, they would never have seen those cars in time. They would have been killed for sure."

"It couldn't happen again," says Verl McManus," "—not without a bunch of people getting killed." He pauses, shaking his head. "I'll tell you that Old Man up there was watching out for all of us that day."

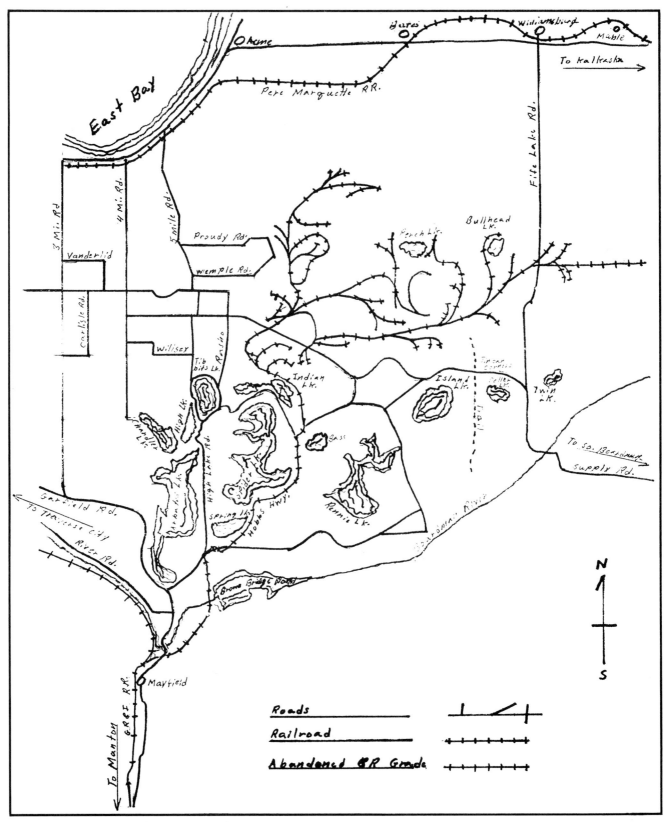

Map of logging railroads in the Boardman River
valley by Robert Winnie.

Old Logging Railroads in the Grand Traverse Region

Among the few vestiges of old logging days in the Grand Traverse area are the miles and miles of abandoned logging railroads, running through the woods from nowhere to nowhere. Only the roadbeds themselves remain, of course, the rails and ties were taken up long ago, but the grades, many of them, are almost perfectly preserved and it gives one a queer feeling to stumble on them unexpectedly in the deep woods, the only sign of man's handiwork for miles around.

They make fine hiking trails if you don't care in particular where you're going.

There are some fine examples in the woods just north of Indian Lake, between Hobbs Highway and Rennie Lake Road. This railroad was built by Cobbs & Mitchell Lumber Company of Cadillac. They carried out exten-sive operations in the Boardman valley, cutting the hardwoods after Perry Hannah had logged off the pines. Cobbs & Mitchell operated mainly on the north side of the Boardman, and their railroad crossed the river on a trestle bridge downstream from Brown Bridge Dam.

Other short line railroad grades abound in the area around Pearl Lake. The timber here was logged off between 1890 and 1910 by the Wilce Lumber Company of Empire. They built a meandering standard gauge line known as the Empire & Southeastern, which connected with the Manistee & Northeastern at Empire Junction north of Honor. It had several branches and spurs.

Two other logging railroads were built in the Glen Lake area. D. H. Day's railroad ran in a curve from the northwest tip of Glen Lake to Glen Haven, where the company had a loading dock. Parts of the old roadbed are still visible. Another short logging line was

New Shay locomotive on North Manitou Island.

operated by the Glen Arbor Lumber Co.; it ran from Glen Lake to the company's dock at Glen Arbor.

Other logging railroads were built in the Kalkaska area by Buckley & Douglas Company, whose Holly Springs RR ran from Antrim (just south of Mancelona) to several camps in Holly Springs Township.

One of the last logging roads to be built in this region was the Manitou Limited on North Manitou Island.

In 1908, two Traverse City men, W. Cary Hull and Frank H. Smith, bought a large tract of hardwood timber on North Manitou. The firm was known as the Smith & Hull Lumber Co. Hull was the son of Henry Hull, founder and president of the Oval Wood Dish Co., one of Traverse City's two largest industries; Smith was a timber cruiser for that firm.

That same year they built a sawmill at the already established village of Crescent on the west side of the island, and completed five miles of logging railroad. In 1909, the company began logging operations on a big scale, hauling its first load of logs to the mill at Crescent City with a second-hand Shay locomotive on July 12. In the fall of that year they bought a second, brand-new "side-winder" from the Lima Locomotive & Machine Works in Ohio, and built three more miles of track. The engine was shipped to Frankfort by rail, then transported to the island on a barge.

In a short while the town of Crescent grew from a mere handful of people to a fair-size settlement of some 300 souls, a hotel, general store, post office, school and saloon. For the next several years the mill was a beehive of activity, processing millions of board feet of lumber for shipment to Chicago and Detroit on passing Lake Michigan steamers. It is said that ships on both north and south bound passage made stops averaging one a day at the company's 600-foot dock.

But the lumber ran out and the mill closed down in 1917. It was dismantled and hauled away, along with the railroad rolling stock and rails. The town that grew up around the mill has long since disappeared, but the railroad beds still remain, running through the woods from nowhere to nowhere.

Old Shay engine on North Manitou.
ROBERT WHITE COLLECTION

First load of logs at Crescent, July 12, 1909.
PIONEER STUDY CENTER

The Manitou Limited, 1910. PIONEER STUDY CENTER

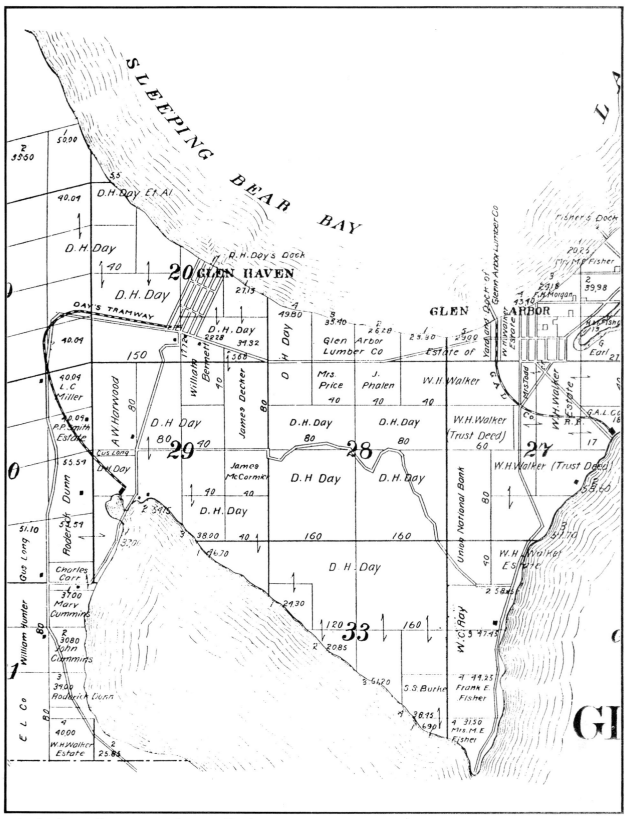

1900 Leelanau County map showing Day's
Tramway and Glen Arbor Railroad.

THIS ENGINE BUILT 1857
STILL IN OPERATION

C.R. WINTERS   Day Saw Mill and Locomotive, Glen Haven, Mich.

EMPIRE TOWNSHIP HERITAGE GROUP

Day's locomotive was on display at Clinch Park,
Traverse City, for many years.
ROBERT WHITE COLLECTION

Day's Mill crew picnic. PIONEER STUDY CENTER

Case's Camp was near O'Neal in Kalkaska
County. MICHIGAN STATE UNIVERSITY HISTORICAL ARCHIVES

The Wonderful One-Hoss Shay

Workhorse of the Woods

Have you heard of the wonderful one-hoss shay
That was built in such a logical way...?
— *OLIVER WENDELL HOLMES*

Of course even the smallest Shay ever built had more horsepower than just one.

But the title is apt in many ways because the Shay was truly the workhorse of the woods in old lumbering days in Michigan and elsewhere. It was powerful, dependable and easy to work with. It could pull as hard as a swayback mule (which it somewhat resembled) and turn in its own length like an Indian pony. And it certainly was built in a very logical way.

In the early days of lumbering in Michigan the timber was cut near a river, then floated downstream to the mill in the spring. Later, as lumbermen had to reach farther and farther away for their timber, the logs were transported to the river or mill on ice-hardened logging roads by horse-drawn drays or sleds. Still later, giant logging wheels were used to half-carry, half-drag the big logs.

By the early 1870s, the cost of transporting logs from stump to mill had risen to $3.50 per thousand board feet — or almost 75% of the total cost of logging. To make matters worse, the bottom fell out of the lumber market in the Panic of 1873, and many Michigan lumbermen were going broke.

It was to meet this challenge that Ephraim Shay, father of the locomotive that bears his name, began to experiment with a logging tramway to cut his transportation costs.

Shay, a young Civil War veteran, came to Michigan from Ohio in 1865, freshly discharged from the army medical corps. For a few years he ran a sawmill in Eaton County, then moved his family to Haring, a tiny settlement just north of Cadillac, hardly more than a clearing in the woods. Here he built a general store and a sawmill, and began logging off the virgin pine on large tracts of timberland between Cadillac and Lake City.

In 1873 he built a wooden tramway from the timber to his mill. It was a primitive affair, with 4 by 4 pine for ties and stringers and maple strips for rails. The logs were drawn on double-truck carriages by teams of horses. Shay found that by this method he could cut his transportation costs in half — $1.25 per thousand. He was prospering while many of his fellow lumbermen were on the verge of bankruptcy.

But the tramway had its problems. On steep grades the heavily loaded cars overran the horses, frequently killing them. Putting brakes on the carriages proved impractical, and for a while the cars were allowed to run free on the downhill slopes. This saved the horses but resulted in many derailments and other mishaps. There had to be a better way.

Shay had an inventive mind and loved fooling around with machinery. Early in 1877 he placed an order for a steam locomotive with William Crippen, a machinist who had recently set up shop at Cadillac. Together the two men built a locomotive largely by hand. It was patterned after the earliest type of steam locomotive to operate on Michigan railroads. It had an upright boiler and two vertical steam cylinders which were connected to two sets of drive-wheels, first by a chain, later by a belt.

The following news item appeared in the Cadillac Weekly News on May 3, 1878:

E. Shay is one of the most enterprising mill men in this section and his mill is in excellent shape, and well equipped. It has a capacity of 25,000 to 30,000 feet a day...

Mr. Shay was the first in this part of the state to employ a locomotive and cars for...lumbering. He has constructed many miles of road at a cost of less than the cost of an ordinary logging road. The gauge is two feet and the track is constructed with solid stringers on ties surmounted with a maple strip.

On this railroad he runs a locomotive constructed by Wm. Crippen & Son of this city. It works well and draws, on two cars, from 4,000 to 5,000 (board feet) a load, making it much cheaper than team work. We enjoyed a trip over a mile or more of road running north from the mill. The course was rough and winding, but grades and curves seemed no obstacles.

The locomotive was a big improvement over horses, but it too had its problems. Shay soon observed that the locomotive, with its more or less rigidly-fixed drive-wheels, chewed up his wooden track unmercifully, especially on curves. This wasn't true, however, of the even heavier flatcars: their flexible, pivoting trucks enabled them to follow the curves and undulations of the primitive roadbed with relatively little damage to the rails.

In a letter to a fellow logger dated October 23, 1888, Shay put his finger on the heart of the problem and its ultimate solution:

"My engine although working successfully is quite different from what I propose to make this winter when I can spare it from the track...Expect to connect my engine to a pair of drivers which shall work on a center same as a truck under an ordinary car. The object is to avoid the friction of a rigid axle on curves which on wood is very great."

Over the next two years Shay tinkered with his locomotive until he got it the way he wanted it. In working out the details he

Shay No. 1884, built 1907 for the Antrim Iron Co. Left to right, Charles Watkins, oiler, Pete Kiel, engineer, and brakeman Melvin Streight, who dressed up for the picture.

invented no new mechanical parts or devices — rather, he used already available components and put them together in a new and ingenious way. The result was a prototype of the unique Shay locomotive which was to become famous as the ideal method of transportation in timber forests and mining fields all over the world — the one and only successful gear-driven locomotive in railroad history.

The original Shay consisted of an upright boiler mounted between two wooden beams that formed the sides of a railroad flatcar. It had two vertical steam cylinders at the side of the boiler. These drove a crankshaft which in turn powered a long pinion shaft extending along the side of the locomotive to its front and rear carriages.

The shaft was made flexible by joining its segments in a clever arrangement of universal joints and sliding couplers. Bevel gears meshed directly with gears on the faces of the wheels. The wheels were deeply flanged on the inner rim to prevent derailment. In later models the boiler was made horizontal and a third cylinder was added for smoother performance.

The essence of Shay's innovation was the limber horizontal shaft with its geared connection to the carriage wheels; this was the invention for which he was granted a patent. It provided a steady, smooth application of power which gave the locomotive its great traction and flexibility. It could go anywhere in the roughest kind of country — dodging stumps, up and down gullies, taking the sharpest turns with ease.

Using the prototype as a model, Carnes, Agerter & Company of Lima, Ohio, built the first Shay locomotive in 1880. This firm, which later developed into the Lima Locomotive & Machine Co., became over the years almost synonymous with the Shay locomotive. Under license by Shay the firm built 2,770 Shay locomotives, of all shapes and sizes, from 1880 to 1945, when the last engine

rolled off the assembly line. They were used all over this country and the world — in such faraway places as Borneo, Chile, Burma and Australia to name just a few.

In his later years Shay wrote an interesting account of his work on the locomotive:

"All of this work was done by me and my mill blacksmith and was crude in the extreme, but it drew my logs from anywhere and all places, saving much labor from teams and was extremely profitable . . .

"My friends remonstrated with me for spending so much time and money on such a crazy idea, and in fact, thought I was a little cracked and did not hesitate to say so. Actually I was tired of it myself, and would have been pleased to give it up, but the constant ridicule to which I was subjected angered me, and I was obliged to continue in self defense and make it a success.

"One consoling feature was, I was all the time making more money from its use and I could get more for my timber than my neighbor mill men. My customers knew rain, bad roads, etc., did not hinder me from logging and their bills would be out on time."

The Shay locomotive made its inventor a wealthy man. In 1888 he moved with his family to Harbor Springs, where he spent the rest of his life. Never one to follow the crowd, he built a house of most unusual design — hexagonal in shape, with six hexagon wings and a tower. It was made of sheet steel, with brick-like stamping on the exterior and other designs within. The house is still in use as a women's apparel shop; it is one of the tourist attractions at Harbor Springs.

Shay also built a short-line railroad to tap the remaining timber resources in the area. After the timber was gone he operated it as a tourist excursion line, hauling sightseers at 25¢ a head. For his Harbor Springs Railroad, later known as Hemlock Central, Shay built three "baby" versions of his locomotive, each an improvement over the one before.

He also tapped the abundant artesian water at Harbor Springs and established the town's first waterworks. Some of the pipe he laid is still in use, but the town has since

117

drilled much deeper artesian wells.

Among his other inventions were a steam-powered railroad tie puller; a device for steering and steadying big ships which is still in use today on ocean-going, oil-drilling platforms; and a pleasure steamboat with a steel hull — it won several races on Little Traverse Bay but had an unfortunate tendency to "submarine" in heavy seas. The boat is on display in a park at Mackinaw City.

Ephraim Shay became one of Harbor Spring's most prominent and best loved citizens. To the children of the village the white-bearded old man was known as Grandpa Shay. They had an especially good reason to remember him with affection. Until his death on April 19, 1916, at 88, Shay devoted his last years to making sleds with clear maple runners which he presented to Harbor Springs children every Christmas. Over the years he made and gave away more than 400 of them.

Big trucks and heavy earth-moving equipment finally brought an end to the dominance of the Shay locomotive in lumbering and mining operations. Of the 2,770 built, it is estimated that no more than 100 are still in existence. Some are still in use, some on exhibit in museums and elsewhere.

One is on display at Town Park in Cadillac. It is a standard gauge locomotive, Shay No. 549, built in 1898, for White & Company of Boyne City. It was operated as Engine No. 3 on the Boyne City & Southeastern RR. Later it was used by other firms, including the Cadillac-Soo Lumber Company, at Sault Ste. Marie.

This sled, on display at Little Traverse Historical Museum, Petoskey, is one of more than 400 Shay built and gave to Harbor Springs children.

118

Shay's all-steel, hexagon-shaped home in
Harbor Springs.

Ephraim Shay in middle age.

Built in 1898 for White & Co., Boyne City,
Shay No. 549 now is on display at Town Park
in Cadillac.

Arcadia and Betsey River Railroad

The name itself is somehow intriguing, conjuring up visions of green Elysian fields and purling brooks. But the Arcadia & Betsey River Railroad was just a fairly typical logging railroad that lasted longer than most.

In the early 1870s a German immigrant named Henry Starke came to a tiny settlement in the northwest corner of Manistee County. He was a builder by trade, a contractor for bridges, harbors and piers. He built a sawmill at the north end of Bar Lake and opened a channel across the sandbar that separated the little lake from Lake Michigan. For several years he cut the big timber near the mill and shipped lumber out on small schooners to Chicago and Milwaukee.

As time went on Starke had to go farther and farther from the mill for his timber, so in 1880 he started building a narrow gauge railroad into the forest. It was a primitive affair with wooden rails, and the engine had an upright boiler. The rails were capped with strap iron about two inches wide.

It was rough country around Arcadia, and the logging road had to cross some steep ravines. There is a picture in the possession of Robert Starke, a grandson of Henry, showing a bridge over one of them. It was 450 feet long and 65 feet high; the rails and ties were supported by huge timbers.

Starke's business boomed and he soon needed a better railroad. In 1893 he formed a corporation of seven stockholders with a capitalization of $123,000. The company was issued a charter in 1895 to operate a standard-gauge railroad from Arcadia to Henry, a distance of 17½ miles. The line was soon completed to Henry, where it linked up with the Chicago & West Michigan; and now Starke could ship his lumber all year around by rail. In 1896 the line was extended to Copemish, where it made junction with the

Sawmill at Arcadia. ROBERT WHITE COLLECTION

Logging train on the Arcadia & Betsey River
Railroad. MICHIGAN STATE UNIVERSITY HISTORICAL ARCHIVES

High Bridge on the A&BR RR.
MICHIGAN STATE HISTORICAL ARCHIVES

Ann Arbor RR and the Manistee & North-eastern. The cost of the entire project was around $150,000.

The railroad's rolling stock consisted at first of one 30-ton locomotive, which was called "The Grasshopper", 15 platform cars, and 35 logging cars. A car known as the "Conductor's Way Car", which was used partly for passengers, was added later. Still later, a full passenger coach with pretty red plush seats was acquired.

Little towns began to spring up along the line. The first was Saile, where the railroad crossed the main highway (now US-31) between Manistee and Traverse City. A sawmill was built here by Hankford and Grund. Later it gave way to a mill that made hardwood butter dishes. It was also a shipping point for all kinds of farm produce — potatoes, apples, grain and even peaches which were shipped in ice-cooled refrigerator cars.

Another early settlement was Malcolm. Here in 1897 a man named Henry Farnsworth built a little store with a post office. People for several miles around would walk to the store and pick up their mail every afternoon when the train dropped it off on its way back to Arcadia. It was also a station for shipping potatoes, beans, apples, cream, pickles and cattle. Old timers tell a story about a runaway cattle car at Malcolm. John Wass was loading cattle for shipment one day when one of the cars broke away and careened down through the valley almost to Arcadia, the cattle bawling and thrashing all the way. The car finally came to a stop and none of the cattle was hurt.

Other tiny villages along the railroad were Sorenson, Butwell, Glowers Lake, Humphrey and Springdale. Nothing is left of them now.

The railroad finally petered out as freight and passenger service disappeared. In its last full year of operation, 1936, passenger revenue was only $3. In 1937 the rails were taken up and sold, the rolling stock moved out, and the Arcadia & Betsey River became a thing of the past.

Engine No. 4 on the A&BR RR.

Logging train on the Bear Lake & Eastern
Railroad, a neighbor of the A&BR RR.
MICHIGAN STATE UNIVERSITY HISTORICAL ARCHIVES

A&BR engine No. 1 at Chicago & West Michigan
crossing, 1895.
MICHIGAN STATE UNIVERSITY HISTORICAL ARCHIVES

Chicago and West Michigan
—Pere Marquette—Chesapeake and Ohio Railroad

Way back in 1872, when the first railroad came to Traverse City, people here were expecting the arrival of another railroad soon.

In a story on January 28, 1872, about the arrival of the Grand Rapids & Indiana Railroad, the *Grand Traverse Herald* announced: "The Lake Shore Railroad will soon be completed to Pentwater, and probably before the close of 1873 will reach Manistee. That it will stop there for any considerable time is not probable. What the northern terminus will be, is, of course, at present unknown. Our friends at Frankfort, Glen Arbor, Leland, and other places along the lake, expect it to follow the shore. If it does, all right; we will rejoice with the people who win; but we, of Traverse City, expect it to come here by a nearly direct route from Manistee. Our faith is very strong, and we wait hopefully for its coming."

Their faith that the railroad would come to Traverse City rather than elsewhere along the lakeshore was confirmed, but they had to wait a very long time for its coming. It was 18 years before the railroad finally reached Traverse City, and by that time it had acquired a different name.

The Michigan Lake Shore Railroad never did reach Manistee; it got no farther north than Pentwater. The Panic of 1873 halted virtually all railroad construction during the seventies, and brought many railroads to the verge of bankruptcy.

In 1881 the Lake Shore merged with three smaller lines to form the Chicago and West Michigan Railway Company. One of these lines was operating a railroad between Grand Rapids and White Cloud. The C&WM completed an extension of this line to Baldwin in 1883, and began to build slowly on to the north, reaching the Manistee River just north of Wellston in 1887. Here it faced a problem of considerable magnitude.

The C&WM's High Bridge over the Manistee was an engineering marvel. It was said to be the longest and finest railroad bridge in the state. The route surveyed for the river crossing followed a line of glacial hills lying roughly north and south. The river had cut a broad deep valley through them, leaving steep sandy bluffs on both sides. The High Bridge (as it was called thereafter) spanned a gap of 1,196 feet and stood 87 feet above the river's high water mark. It was built of heavy timbers that rested on 58 stone-and-concrete piers. The work was done by Vincent Brothers of Grand Rapids, and it was finished in 1889.

Railroad construction went forward while the bridge was being built, the route north having already been surveyed, partly cleared and graded. By 1889 the road had passed through Kaleva and Thompsonville and was approaching Interlochen. Meanwhile, the surveyors had completed their work on the route to Traverse City and were working to the east on an extension of the line to Charlevoix and Petoskey, with a branch to Elk Rapids. On April 10, 1890, this item appeared in the *Grand Traverse Herald*:

The right of way has been secured between Elk Rapids and Traverse City. The Chicago and West Michigan has assured Elk Rapids that it would commence building when it was secured. Elk Rapids will have rails by July. How are you, Traverse City? Elk Rapids Progress.

Quite well, thank you, and we are glad to see you so hearty.

Traverse City people had been following the progress of the railroad with great interest, and when it reached town in June of 1890 — coming up from the south on the

Grand Traverse Herald, Sept. 16, 1897.

opposite bank of the Boardman River from the GR&I — there was general rejoicing.

The village put on a gala celebration to welcome the arrival of the first C&WM passenger train on Sunday, July 8. A special train carrying 100 Traverse City citizens and a brass band on gaily-decorated flatcars pulled out at five o'clock in the afternoon to meet the incoming train at Beitner, the first station south of Traverse City. The inbound passenger train carried officials of the C&WM, including C. M. Heald, General Manager; J. K. Agnew, General Superintendent; and Captain W. A. Gavett, General Passenger Agent.

The two trains pulled up head to head at Beitner, and both official parties alighted to exchange greetings and congratulations while the crowd cheered and the band played. Later, as the trains drew near to Traverse City, the bluffs on both sides of the Boardman River were lined with people cheering and waving hats and handkerchiefs. The trains circled the river bed and drew up at the GR&I station between the river and the bay, to be met by even larger crowds.

That same day a new excursion boat docked at Traverse City. She was the *Charles McVae*, owned by the Chicago & West Michigan and skippered by Captain R. C. Britten. A steamer of 260 tons, with accommodations for 500 people, she would open a regular summer schedule between Traverse City and Mackinac Island.

For a few months, while its new depot was being built, the C&WM used a small building just west of the GR&I station, near the spot where the Morgan Cider Factory was to stand. A prominent Traverse City builder, Arthur W. Wait (nephew of S. E. Wait) had been awarded the contract for all railroad buildings between Traverse City and Baldwin, 40 in all. They included depots, section houses, engine houses, handcar and tool houses. Wait purchased all materials in Traverse City and employed between 40 and 50 local workers.

He finished the passenger depot, and a freight station, in the fall of 1890. The passenger depot stood just east of Union Street, just south of, and adjacent to the Hannah, Lay grist mill. The freight station still stands on the corner of Cass and Lake. The passenger depot cost $2,500, the freight house $1,200. Wait also built an engine house with seven stalls at the freight yard south of town on Boardman Lake.

The ten-mile branch line to Elk Rapids was finished in 1890, and the main line extension from Traverse City to Petoskey, a distance of 78.5 miles, was completed by 1894.

On July 20, 1890, the C&WM issued its first Traverse City timetable. Trains would leave Traverse City at 8:30 a.m. and 3:20 p.m., arriving at Chicago at 11:35 p.m. and 8:05 a.m. Passenger coaches and Pullmans were transferred and attached to Michigan Central trains at New Buffalo. As the summer traffic from the north grew heavier, however, the cars were pulled into Chicago as separate trains, cutting travel time by one hour.

At the same time, the C&WM announced that it had just purchased 10 deluxe new Pullman cars, four of which would be used on the Traverse City run. They were 65 feet long and painted a wine dark red on the outside. The interiors were finished in solid antique oak and the seats were upholstered in old gold plush. All the windows were of heavy plate glass, and the cars were lighted by 4 powerful double lamps (8 burners), making the interior as light as day. There was a gentlemen's dressing room at one end, and a ladies room at the other. Both had marble-top washstands and large plateglass mirrors. The cars were heated by steam; opposite the ladies dressing room there was a zinc-lined room with a Baker heater in case the steam heat was inadequate.

In 1889 the C&WM leased a 33-mile line from the Grand Rapids, Kalkaska and South

Eastern Railroad. It ran from Rapid City to Stratford in the northeast corner of Missaukee County. Among the settlements along the way were Ricker, Mahan, Kalkaska, Sharon and Halstead — most of which are no longer in existence. A short logging spur on this line ran from Mahan, just north of Kalkaska, to the vicinity of the Guernsey Lakes.

In the summer of 1905 the agent at South Boardman got a wire from the train dispatcher at Barker Creek that there was trouble on the Mahan branch. A farmer named John Brown had torn up the track and had built a rail fence across it. He had also felled a large tree across the line and was sitting in the upper branches with a Winchester rifle, drawing a bead up and down the track. The South Boardman agent notified the sheriff, who paid a call on Brown and persuaded him to get down from his perch and remove the tree.

Brown had been giving the railroad trouble for some time. A few years earlier he had started to build a house across the railroad right of way. His grievance was that when he bought the farm nobody told him anything about the railroad right of way. He wanted the railroad to pay up, or else. Needless to say, the railroad came out on top of that dispute; Brown put up a good fight but lost the battle.

Traverse City people had just gotten used to calling the railroad the Chicago & West Michigan when the name was changed again. In 1899 the C&WM was consolidated with the Flint & Pere Marquette and the Detroit, Grand Rapids & Western to form the Pere Marquette Railroad. The Pere Marquette it was to remain until 1951, when it became part of the Chesapeake & Ohio system; so people who remember the railroad in its early days, remember it as the Pere Marquette.

The railroad did a thriving business during the early decades of the 20th century. In the first 10 months of 1926, for example, its

gross earnings were $38,500,000 in freight, $4,000,000 in passenger service. In that year the Pere Marquette built a new depot on Boardman Lake at a cost of $75,000. It was described by the *Record-Eagle* as being of the "umbrella type of architecture so popular in the west." Railroad officials who came up for the dedication ceremonies on January 6, 1927, claimed there was no finer station anywhere along the line.

At a ceremonial dinner at the Park Place, General Freight Agent George Hart reminisced about the early days. "I well remember the old days when the Pere Marquette first started in Traverse City. At first we had no building. Then we secured one where the Morgan Plant now stands.

"In 1891 we occupied for the first time our old passenger depot that we have now abandoned. I sold the first ticket ever sold out of that station. I sold it to one of the Grand Traverse region's noblemen, William Beitner. He bought a 1,000-mile book for $20.

"The population of Traverse City in 1890 was 4,000. In 1894 it was 9,000, and that shows what a bang-up good railroad will do for a community."

Business began to fall off sharply in the late nineteen-twenties, and in July of 1930 the PM cut passenger service from four trains north and south each day to only one through train. At the same time it announced there would be no sleeper service during the winter.

Business picked up during the war years but then slumped badly in its aftermath. In 1954 the C&O established a new route to the south by abandoning the 36-mile line from Kaleva to Baldwin. The C&O now ran over the old Manistee & Northeastern tracks from Kaleva to Manistee, giving that city a resumption of railroad passenger service after a lapse of 24 years.

Passenger service to Traverse City ended in 1966. On Saturday morning, October 29, the last passenger train pulled out of the

Peck's imaginary PM depot: it was planned but never built.
The rest of the picture is factual, including the PM eating house at right center.

Pere Marquette depot at Williamsburg.

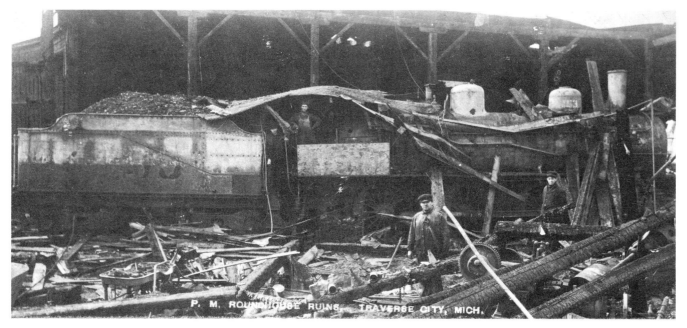

PM roundhouse after fire on March 10, 1907.
PIONEER STUDY CENTER

PM train with boxcars of canned cherries.
PIONEER STUDY CENTER

Boardman Lake station. The single coach was crowded, mostly by railroad buffs eager to make a last nostalgic run on the railroad. In the fall of 1979 the C&O petitioned the ICC for permission to abandon the line from Traverse City to Manistee.

One of the thrills of riding the C&O from Traverse City to Chicago in the late nineteen-forties and early fifties (the trip took almost 15 hours) was crossing High Bridge, the 1196-foot span, 87 feet high, over the Manistee River. The bridge was so shaky by that time that the engineer had to slow down to five miles an hour, and the train crept across at that almost imperceptible pace. But the eeriest part of it was looking down at the river from the passenger coach window. You couldn't see any part of the bridge from that perspective, and it seemed as though the train was suspended in thin air.

Built in 1888, the bridge was dismantled in 1955, a year after the C&O changed its route and abandoned the track between Kaleva and Baldwin.

Pere Marquette High Bridge over Manistee River, Forty Miles South of Traverse City, Mich. Length 1170 feet. Height 96 feet.

High Bridge, highest in Michigan, near Manistee, Mich.

COPYRIGHTED BY ORSON W. PECK, TRAVERSE CITY, MICH.

The High Bridge, Northern Division
of the Pere Marquette R. R.

PM engine at Boardman roundhouse.
ARLIE KILLMAN COLLECTION

PM engine. ARLIE KILLMAN COLLECTION

Wreck on the Pere Marquette, March 21, 1904,
near Kalkaska. Several injuries, no fatalities.

Clearing Wreck on P.M.R.R.
Mar 22. '04

Photo by
Beebe, Kalkaska

Unidentified wreck on the PM. PIONEER STUDY CENTER

Wreck scene on P.M. R.R.
Mar, 23, '04   -II-   Photo by Beebe, Kalkaska

Wreck scene on P.M.R.R
Mar., 23, '04   -III-   Photo by Beebe, Kalkaska,

Wreck scene on P. M. R. R.   Photo by

Wreck on the Pere Marquette at Beitner

Six people died in the worst train wreck in Traverse City history because five men, who were responsible, all had a simultaneous lapse of memory. Of those five, three paid the extreme penalty. It happened on Wednesday, August 20, 1919.

Pere Marquette No. 6, southbound, left the Union Street station at Traverse City on schedule at 11:30 in the morning. Engineer Fletcher Gage, formerly of Traverse City but now a resident of Grand Rapids, was hauling a light load of passenger coaches. His fireman was Earl Beeman, also of Grand Rapids.

No. 6 passed the Boardman yards south of town at 11:32, exactly on time. It proceeded south along the Boardman River valley toward Beitner, gradually picking up speed. Speed was necessary to climb Grawn Hill, after making the big curve to the west just below Beitner.

At 11:31, precisely one minute before the passenger train passed Boardman, extra train No. 362, through freight from Grand Rapids, was reported at Grawn, travelling slowly. The telegraph operator there expected the freight to stop and back into a siding, clearing the track for No. 6. Instead, it kept on going, picking up speed as it approached the steep grade into the river valley. From that moment on, No. 362 was in deadly peril. So, for that matter, was No. 6.

Freight 362 was also a fairly light train, hauling a string of coal cars. It had a crew of five: engineer Earl G. Eighmy, fireman Guy L. Shenneman, conductor Fred S. Neubecker, and brakemen F. J. Davis and Roy Peets, all of Grand Rapids. Eighmy had a spotless record of 15 years with the railroad. Shenneman had been called back to work by the Pere Marquette a few days previously; he had been working as a streetcar conductor in Detroit. F. J. Davis was new with the company; he had been working only a few weeks and was still on half pay.

Suddenly a thought flashed through conductor Neubecker's mind, a thought that chilled him to the bone. The crew had forgotten that passenger train! At almost the same instant, as he testified before a coronor's jury two days later, there was a terrific crash as the two engines hit head-on.

According to witnesses, the two engines were thrown at least forty feet into the air. There was no explosion because the boilers of both engines remained intact, but one of the steam pipes snapped, letting loose a three-inch jet of steam with a scream and whistle that could be heard for miles. Strangely enough, there was no tremendous jar throughout the length of the trains. Neubecker and Peets, who had been looking forward out of windows on opposite sides of the caboose, were not even thrown to the floor. Railroad officials later agreed that if the trains had been heavy ones, they would have been entirely wrecked.

But it was bad enough. The two engines,

PM wreck at Beitner, Aug. 21, 1919.
ARLIE KILLMAN COLLECTION

Beitner wreck. ARLIE KILLMAN COLLECTION

with tenders telescoped into the cabs, came down beside the tracks one on top of the other — a smoking, seeething, hissing mass of twisted steel. So great was the impact that one 400-pound piece of frame was hurled 200 feet to the bank of the Boardman River. Also telescoped into the tender and engine was the mail and baggage car of No. 6. Many of the coal cars were derailed, spewing tons of coal over the right of way. But the passenger coaches had remained on the rails and only a few of the passengers were injured — cuts, bruises, nothing serious. They were loaded aboard the coaches and taken by another engine back to Traverse City, where the injured were rushed in ambulances to Johnson Hospital. The absence of casualties among the passengers was attributed to the facts that the train was lightly loaded and that the coaches were made of steel.

Meanwhile, the bodies of six trainmen were somewhere in that mass of tons of twisted steel, and the grim task of finding them went forward. A wrecking crane and a crew of men reached the scene by early afternoon and began the job of clearing the right of way. Doctors and nurses had been summoned to the wreck, and a temporary telegraph station was set up on the spot.

Four of the bodies were recovered that afternoon. Most were crushed and mutilated almost beyond recognition. The body of Fletcher Gage, engineer of the passenger train, was found beneath the engine tender. That of Frank W. Cushman, of Petoskey, a mail clerk on the passenger train, was found beneath the freight engine, as was the body of freight brakeman F. J. Davis. Earl Beeman, the passenger fireman, was still alive when pulled from the wreckage, but he was scalded

Beitner wreck, Boardman River in background.
ARLIE KILLMAN COLLECTION

from head to foot, great patches of skin being burned from his body, and died that afternoon at General Hospital. He was a widower with four small children, his wife having died in December from influenza.

In a scene reminiscent of Dante's Inferno, the railroad crew labored all night clearing the track and searching for the bodies of the two missing trainmen. They worked by the ghastly light of acetylene torches and intermitent flashes of lightning. Despite frequent thundershowers, a crowd of several hundred people kept a ghoulish vigil all night, crowding forward as each piece of wreckage was removed by the crane, in the expectation of seeing one of the bodies.

The bodies of freight engineer Earl G. Eighmy and his fireman Guy Shenneman were not recovered until Friday afternoon, after tons of coal, twisted metal and other debris had been removed from the right of way. Shenneman's body was so horribly mangled that identification was possible only because two fingers were missing on his right hand — the result of an accident years before.

Freight conductor Fred S. Neubecker and brakeman Roy Peets told virtually the same story in their testimony before a coroner's jury on Friday. Until that flash of memory of Neubecker's just before the crash, all of the crew had forgotten about the passenger train. With tears rolling down his cheeks Neubecker told coroner E. B. Minor:

"I tell you, we simply forgot about the passenger train. We should have known." He reached into his pocket and pulled out some papers. "There's our time-table and here's my watch," he said. "It was our business to keep out of the way of the passenger train. And it was the first thing I've had against me in 28 years of service on the railroad."

He volunteered to remain at Traverse City as a witness, but said that if the coroner did not need him now, he would like to go to his family.

E. E. Cain, general superintendent of the Pere Marquette, Grand Rapids, arrived on Thursday morning and took charge of the wrecking crew operation. Interviewed by a *Record-Eagle* reporter, he said that the freight crew was entirely to blame for the accident.

"There is only one cause," he said. "The freight crew overlooked the passenger train. The freight should have headed in at Grawn, but neglected to comply with this order."

J. J. Hayes, general superintendent of the PM at Detroit, followed Cain to the scene of the wreck on Friday morning. Asked about responsibility for the tragedy, he said:

"The crew forgot. That was all. South and east are superior bound trains. That means they have rights over north and west trains. This particular freight was an extra, and had no rights at all. The men of the crew simply forgot that a passenger train was due."

Asked if the freight train might have tried to beat the passenger train, he said, "There was no earthly chance of this. The men, if they had looked at their time-tables and watches, would have known they were in danger the moment they left Grawn. It would have been suicide to have tried to beat the passenger. There is no chance that they tried to do this."

How did it happen? How did five men, most of them veteran railroaders, completely forget something so important, a matter of life and death? No one knows. No one will ever know.

There was one other eerie aspect of the tragic affair. Frank W. Cushman, 38, the mail clerk who was instantly killed in the crash, is reported to have said a strange thing as he left his rooming house in Grand Rapids on his last trip north.

"Goodbye," he told his landlady at 61½ Lagrave Ave. S. E. "My home is in heaven." No one afterward could figure out what he meant.

Wreck at Grawn, April 5, 1904. Two freight
trains hit head on. Crews jumped to safety
before collision. PIONEER STUDY CENTER

Unidentified wreck on PM, early 1900s.
PIONEER STUDY CENTER

P.M. WRECK MABLE. MICH. JULY. 19, 1910

Brakeman Walter Beeman was killed and six trainmen were injured when two freight trains met head on at Mabel.

P.M. WRECK. MABLE. MICH. JULY, 19 1910.

145

Loading logs on the M&NE. DAVID C. WERLY COLLECTION

Manistee & Northeastern

When the first Manistee & Northeastern train pulled into the depot grounds in Traverse City on the morning of June 29, 1892, only a small crowd was waiting to greet her. Traverse City people could perhaps be excused for not showing greater enthusiasm. They had understandably grown a bit blase' about railroads, since the M&NE was, after all, only the third railroad to reach town. "No big deal," they might have said, if that expression had been current then, which it wasn't. Still and all, Traverse City, like Copemish, now had the services of three railroad lines, and that was something to be proud of, at least.

The president of the M&NE was aboard that first train, along with other railroad officials, and if Edward Buckley was disap-

pointed in the size of the crowd, he didn't say so. He made a little speech, saying that plans had been approved to build a fine new depot of brick and stone on this very spot. It would cost twice as much as any other in the city and would be "correspondingly handsomer."

Buckley said he was doing this because of the generous way the company had been treated by local citizens, who had purchased the rights of way from Carp Lake to Traverse City; and by Hannah, Lay & Company, which had donated the dock front and depot grounds, worth at least $10,000.

"We expect shortly two new cars that we ordered some time ago," he went on to say. "One is a first-class, 60-foot car that is equal to the best of the Chicago & West Michigan. At one end will be a smoking room where passengers who indulge in the weed may retire and enjoy a smoke, without going into

Loading potatoes at the M&NE depot in Traverse City. Station agent Allen S. Barber is first on left of the three men on the station platform. He was succeeded as agent by John Jenks. PIONEER STUDY CENTER

M. & N.E. Station.

Manistee and Northern R. R. Station, Traverse City, Mich.

PIONEER STUDY CENTER

148

the regular smoker. The other is a combination baggage and passenger coach."

Regular passenger service began on July 4, and the time schedule was printed in the *Grand Traverse Herald*. It called for two trains daily between Traverse City and Manistee, with intermediate stops at Hatch's Crossing, Carp Lake (Fouch), Solon, Cedar Run, Lake Ann and Interlochen. One would leave Traverse City at 9:45 a.m. and arrive at Manistee at 12:20. The other would leave Traverse City at 4:10 in the afternoon and arrive at Manistee at 7:20.

Return trips would leave Manistee at 6:35 in the morning and 1:40 in the afternoon, reaching Traverse City at 9:05 a.m. and 4:10 p.m.

The new service was especially welcome to people living in the Lake Ann - Interlochen area and in Leelanau County. At about this same time, a new steamboat, "Sally" — Morgan Cummings, master —began operating a passenger service on Lake Leelanau between Leland and Fouch, with stops at Provemont (now Lake Leelanau) and Bingham

Landing. Leelanau County people could now make connections with the M&NE at Fouch, spend seven hours in Traverse City and return the same night. Skipper Cummings would also take fishing parties out on the lake while waiting for the train.

The Manistee & Northeastern was only four years old when it reached Traverse City. In 1887 the Manistee firm of Buckley & Douglas bought the sawmill, timber lands and logging railroad of Nuttal and Rudock and rebuilt the mill and modernized it with the latest equipment. In 1888 the company began to build a standard gauge railroad into its timber holdings to the north and east.

By the end of that year the railroad had reached Lemon Lake (half way between Kaleva and Copemish), a distance of 28 miles, having crossed the tracks of the Chicago & West Michigan railroad at Kaleva. Next year, construction was completed to Copemish, where junction was made with the Toledo & Ann Arbor — then on to Lake Ann in 1890, crossing the C&WM tracks again at Interlochen.

Here the timber was so plentiful that the

M&NE depot at Traverse City. PIONEER STUDY CENTER

First depot at Lake Ann.

company was in no hurry to press on, and it was almost two years before the final leg of 17 miles to Traverse City was finished. Passenger service had been opened in January, 1899; a time schedule issued on April 28 of that year shows two trains operating daily except Sunday between Manistee and Lemon Lake via Onekama.

Meanwhile the railroad had built branch lines to Onekama, Bear Creek and Twin Lake; also from Platte River Junction to Honor and Empire Junction, where it connected with the Empire & Southeastern railroad. Short branches were built, too, from Copemish to Henry, where connection was made with the Arcadia & Betsey River railroad; and from Solon to Cedar. Later, the Cedar branch was extended to Provemont (1903); and in 1910 a long branch line was built from the main line just north of Kaleva to Grayling, a distance of almost 80 miles.

The railroad did a brisk business in its early years. In 1890, for example, it carried a total of 117,040 tons, of which 99 percent was forest products. In 1891 freight shipments included 125,000,000 feet of lumber, 75,000 shingles, 2,000,000 cedar posts, 30,000 cords of bark, and 10,000 cords of firewood. It also carried more than 50,000 passengers.

Thriving communities sprang up along the line. Among them were Nessen City, Buckley (where Buckley & Douglas operated a big sawmill under lease), Interlochen, Lake Ann and Copemish, which in 1900 had a population of almost 1,000, 30 business establishments, a hotel and an opera house.

Although the number of passengers continued to increase until it reached a peak of 190,000 in 1915, freight loadings had begun to fall off in the early 1900s. It had been hoped that, as the timber ran out, farm produce would take up the slack in freight,

M&NE logging train near Solon.
MICHIGAN STATE UNIVERSITY HISTORICAL ARCHIVES

M&NE section crew near Platte River Junction.
MICHIGAN STATE UNIVERSITY HISTORICAL ARCHIVES

and the railroad did its best to encourage farming on its depleted timber land. But it didn't work out that way. There was only a thin layer of fertile topsoil in the former forest land, and it too was depleted after two or three crops. The railroad carried 17,156 tons of farm produce in 1903 and 42,849 in 1916. By 1919, however, the number had dropped to 27,560 tons.

The railroad got a new lease on life beginning in 1910, when the River Branch to Grayling was completed. Here Buckley & Douglas, and Louis Sands, had acquired between 300,000,000 and 400,000,000 feet of virgin timber, and logging operations in that area sustained the company for a few more years.

By 1917, however, the railroad was clearly in deep financial trouble. After a few months of operation under the federal government during the War, the railroad went into bankruptcy in 1918. Buckley & Douglas was dealt another heavy blow in 1920 when its sawmill, salt plant and railroad shops burned down in the second biggest fire in Manistee history. The Manistee River branch line to Grayling was abandoned in 1924.

The Manistee & Northeastern was taken over by the Pere Marquette in 1932. In 1934 the main line from Kaleva to Solon was abandoned, and on September 14 of that year, the railroad's freight and passenger offices in Traverse City were moved to the old Pere Marquette depot on Cass Street. (The Pere Marquette had built a new depot on Boardman Lake in 1926.) The M&NE depot was leased for storage for a few years, then torn down in the 1940s.

Under Pere Marquette ownership the railroad continued to operate the branch line

Loading logs on the M&NE.
MICHIGAN STATE UNIVERSITY HISTORICAL ARCHIVES

Copemish depot.
MICHIGAN STATE UNIVERSITY HISTORICAL ARCHIVES

MICHIGAN STATE UNIVERSITY HISTORICAL ARCHIVES

from Solon to Provemont, and the TCL&M line from Traverse City to Northport via Hatch's Crossing. But in 1944 the ten miles of the Provemont branch was abandoned, and the last freight train made its run in April of that year.

Many Traverse area people were saddened by the passing of the Manistee & Northeastern; it had for so long been a part of their lives. Among them was Editor Jay P. Smith, who wrote a requiem for the railroad in the *Record-Eagle* in 1934.

People would remember the many thousands of logs that had hummed over its tracks, he wrote, starting with the tag end of the Betsie River pine and ending with the last of the hardwoods. It had been a proud railroad in its day, providing the connecting link between Manistee and Traverse City, two good lumber towns.

But what they would remember best, he thought, was the social activities — the great summer excursion trains that carried thousands of Traverse City people to Manistee, and thousands of Manistee people to Traverse City. And then there were the hunting trains in the fall.

"One Sunday morning a whole lot of years ago," he wrote, "the excursion train pulled out of Traverse City with 68 hunting dogs in the baggage car, and hunters and their dogs were dropped off from Hatch's Crossing to Kaleva and picked up again that night when the excursion returned. Some place about the city are pictures of the hunters and their dogs lined up before the train started.

Depot, Platte River Junction. Mich.

Section crew at Platte River Junction.

"Such splendid wing shots as Bill Bowen, Bill Murrell, Harry Alley, Charles Carver and Fred Curtis were usually on hand when the Sunday train pulled out in bird season. Dr. Demas Cochlin delivering his Sunday sermon heard the imaginary whir of wings and gave thought to his hunting companions on those days.

"Now the railroad has been taken over by the Pere Marquette, but the bigger system will never be able to swallow up the memories of the M&NE, which, as the loggers used to say, might not be so very long, but she was just as wide as any railroad."

Section crew at Honor depot.

Passenger Depot, Honor, Mich.

M&NE wreck near Nessen City.

Ann Arbor Railroad and Car Ferries

The first cross-lake ferry service was established by the Toledo Ann Arbor and North Michigan Railroad (later known as the Ann Arbor) in 1892. On November 24 of that year, the car ferry *Ann Arbor No. 1* made the first crossing from Frankfort to Kewaunee, Wis., carrying four carloads of coal.

Prior to that time, freight was shipped across Lake Michigan from Frankfort, Ludington and Muskegon to Wisconsin ports and Chicago on "break-bulk" steamers. In this kind of operation, package freight was transferred from railroad car to ferry and off-loaded the same way, a tedious and costly procedure.

James M. Ashley, former territorial governor of Montana, had a better idea. Ashley was a promoter of vision and daring. A big man, six feet tall and heavy, with a shock of prematurely white hair, Ashley had boundless energy and a good head for figures. He reasoned that much time and money could be saved by transporting the railroad cars themselves aboard ship. (This, of course, was already being done by ferries across the Niagara, St. Lawrence, Detroit and St. Clair rivers and the eight-mile-wide Straits of Mackinac; but a ferry across a large body of open water such as Lake Michigan represented a major innovation, a whole new ballgame.)

Ashley seems to have had a cross-lake ferry operation in mind as early as 1877, when he acquired an unfinished railroad, the

First train into Benzonia, July 1899.

Annarbor Car Ferry No. 1. This boat was the first of a large fleet of car ferries that now ply the open waters on the Great Lakes

Car ferry *No. 1 or 2,* Hotel Frontenac at rear.

160

Ann Arbor & Toledo, which had gone bankrupt in the Panic of 1873. With the help of his two sons, James Jr. and Harry, who even were taller than their father and just as energetic, Ashley completed the railroad to Toledo in 1879 and then began to build northward from Ann Arbor.

The Ashleys were perennially short of money, and in addition to daring and imagination they seem to have used a good deal of high-handedness in building their railroad. In some cases where they couldn't obtain rights of way, they simply pushed on through and worried about lawsuits later. Some local construction contractors had to wait a long time for their money; some apparently were never paid at all. James Ashley Jr. said later that he could write a book entitled, "How to Build 600 Miles of Railroad without a Damned Cent." (The Ashleys built other railroads in Michigan, too.)

In 1888 the railroad had reached the Manistee River valley, and Ashley toyed briefly with the idea of terminating the line at Manistee. He negotiated for the purchase of the Manistee & Northeastern Railroad or at least the use of their tracks into that city; at that time the M&NE had reached a point three miles north of Kaleva, some 28 miles from Manistee. But Ashley couldn't get the deal he wanted and decided to push on north — after threatening to run a separate line into Manistee.

In 1889 the railroad reached Copemish; and in the following year an independent line, the Frankfort & South Eastern, also arrived there. In 1892 Ashley acquired the F&SE and thus brought the entire railroad from Toledo to Frankfort under his control.

That same year Ashley built a ferry slip and other facilities at Elberta, across Betsie Lake from Frankfort, and ordered a pair of car ferries from the Craig Ship Building Company of Toledo. *Ann Arbor No. 1* was launched on September, 1892, and went into service, as previously noted, on November 24 of that year. Her sister ship, *Ann Arbor No. 2,* reached Elberta on New Year's Eve and was put in service almost immediately.

Both were wooden ships, almost identical in design. Both had four tracks, with a capacity of 24 railroad cars and, like the *St. Ignace* at the Straits of Mackinac, they had triple propellers — two at the stern and one at the bow. The bow propeller had proved useful in breaking sheet ice at the Straits, but it was not effective on the lake and was soon removed from both Ann Arbor boats.

As business prospered, the Ann Arbor added a third ship, *Ann Arbor No. 3,* to its fleet in 1898. She was the first steel ferry, with a double hull, and she proved to be the most durable and dependable of all Ann Arbor ferries, serving faithfully until she was retired in 1960.

Ann Arbor No. 4, launched in 1906, was the "jinx ship" of the fleet, as capricious and accident-prone as her sister No. 3 was dependable. She became legendary for her mishaps. The most serious of these was in 1909 when she capsized and turned on her side at Manistique as a result of faulty loading; and in 1923, when, after battling the great storm of February 13, she went aground and piled up against the breakwater at Elberta.

Although the Ann Arbor was mainly a freight line, its passenger traffic began to increase dramatically as the tourist and summer resort industry opened up in northern Michigan around the turn of the century. It was to boost this business that the Ann Arbor built a plush resort hotel, the Royal Frontenac, in Frankfort, in 1901.

The Royal Frontenac was one of the great luxurious summer hotels of its time — comparable in every way to the Grand Hotel on Mackinac Island, which had been built in 1887 by two other railroads, the Grand Rapids & Indiana and the Michigan Central, with a Cleveland steamship company. It was a white, green-trimmed, three-story building,

Unlucky *No. 4* on her side at Manistique, May
29, 1909.

No. 4 aground at Frankfort pier, Feb. 14, 1923.

500 feet long and 100 feet wide. Each of its 225 guest rooms had electricity, plumbing, hot water and a telephone. Black students from Fisk University in Tennessee served as porters and waiters. Available to hotel guests were horseback riding lessons, boat excursions and swimming instruction.

The Hotel was kept full all season by the railroad's "Resort Special", which rolled in every day with coachloads of summer people from Ohio, Indiana and Illinois. Although it originally stayed open year around, it closed up for the winter beginning in 1907. The Hotel burned to the ground on the night of January 12, 1912, and was never rebuilt.

At peak service during the early 1900s, the Ann Arbor ran two passenger trains daily (Sundays were excepted later). Early every

morning, train No. 52 would pull out of Elberta and go past the Y at the southeast end of Betsie Lake, then chug backwards to the Frankfort depot (near Hotel Frontenac), load up with passengers and head south. At about the same time, No. 51 would leave Toledo and head north, arriving at Elberta-Frankfort late in the afternoon. The two trains would pass each other somewhere around Alma or Mt. Pleasant. They carried a baggage coach, a combination mail and smoker car, two or three standard day coaches and a parlor car and diner.

The Resort Specials were plushier. They consisted of Pullman sleepers and an opulent diner (with silver service and real linen on the table), as well as baggage and mail coaches. Until the time of the first World War, the

Resort train at Beulah, Aug. 14, 1910.
MICHIGAN STATE UNIVERSITY HISTORICAL ARCHIVES

Early station at Benzonia, 1890.
MICHIGAN STATE UNIVERSITY HISTORICAL ARCHIVES

Ann Arbor and M&NE depots at Thompsonville.
MICHIGAN STATE UNIVERSITY HISTORICAL ARCHIVES

Ann Arbor also ran a daily-except-Sunday train between Frankfort and Cadillac. It left Cadillac at 9:45 in the morning and reached Frankfort around noon; then headed back to Cadillac at 3:45 in the afternoon.

Then there was the famous train called "Ping Pong". It began as a convenience for Royal Frontenac guests, just an engine and one car running from the hotel to a golf course on the east end of Frankfort. Later it shuttled for many years between Frankfort and Beulah, sometimes going as far as Thompsonville. Since there was no way to turn around at Beulah, the Ping Pong had to make the return trip to Frankfort in reverse. As historian Leonard Case says in his book on Benzie County, many Benzie people got their first train ride as children aboard the Ping Pong.

Meanwhile, its ferry business flourishing, the Ann Arbor added new routes to its schedule and boats to its fleet. In 1894 it opened a regular run to Menominee, and in 1895 one to Gladstone, with a passenger stop at Escanaba. In 1896 a triangular service from Elberta to Kewaunee and Manitowoc was established; this was later changed to a separate run for Manitowoc. In 1902, service to Gladstone was shifted permanently to Manistique.

Ann Arbor No. 5 was built in 1910. At 360 feet she was the longest car ferry on Lake Michigan at that time — 100 feet longer than Ann Arbor No. 4. Her powerful, 3000 horsepower, triple-expansion engines made her the champion ice breaker of the Ann Arbor fleet.

Ann Arbor No. 2 was retired in 1913 and sold to the Manistee Iron Works, which reduced her to a barge. *Ann Arbor No. 1* burned to the water's edge at Manitowoc in 1919; her hull was recovered and turned into a barge.

Ping Pong at Beulah. 25¢ per trip to Frankfort.
MICHIGAN STATE UNIVERSITY HISTORICAL ARCHIVES

To replace these boats, the Ann Arbor had *No. 6* built in 1916 and *No. 7* in 1924. Shortly after the launching of *Ann Arbor No. 7*, the Ann Arbor Railroad came under control of the Wabash Railroad; and the last new ship built for the Ann Arbor was launched in 1927 and named the *Wabash.* She had engines very similar to *No. 6* and *No. 7*, but was about 20 feet longer.

The 1920s were peak years for the Ann Arbor car ferries. In 1925, for example they handled 80,272 cars, as compared with 32,297 in 1910. Business declined in the Depression years, however, and except for the heavy traffic of the war years, continued to fall off through the Fifties and Sixties.

The 1920s were peak years also for passenger traffic on the Ann Arbor Railroad. In 1920 it carried 617,533 passengers. Together with freight loadings, however, the number of passengers decreased sharply with the growing popularity of the automobile in the thirties. The last passenger train pulled out of the Frankfort station on July 19, 1950. It carried mostly railroad buffs, eager to ride the last passenger train on the Ann Arbor Railroad.

Passenger traffic aboard the Ann Arbor car ferries was never more than a small fraction of the Pere Marquette's at Ludington. But, beginning in the 1930s, the number of vacationing passengers with their automobiles increased steadily. In 1960, for example, Ann Arbor ferries carried 13,436 passengers and 4,882 accompanied autos. As it was with the railroads, however, passenger service on the ferries was marginally profitable at best.

Freight loadings and passenger service on the car ferries began to fall off during the

1960s. For lack of traffic the run to Manistique was abandoned in 1968, and in 1970 service to Menominee was discontinued.

Ann Arbor No. 6, altered in 1959, became the *Arthur K. Atkinson,* after the president of the Wabash Railroad System. *No. 5* was scrapped in the early sixties. The *Wabash* was rebuilt in 1963 and converted from coal to oil firing. Her deck was raised to accommodate auto frames on flat cars. After the work was finished, she was renamed *City of Green Bay;* but in 1972 her coast guard certificate was permitted to expire. She was laid up at Frankfort until 1974, when she was sold to a salvage firm in Ontario. Later she was loaded with scrap, towed to Spain and cut up.

No. 7 was rebuilt in 1965 and her name was changed to *Viking.* She was given four new diesel-electric engines and a bow thruster for greater maneuverability; total cost of the conversion was 2.5 million dollars.

During the five-year period from 1973 to 1978, the Ann Arbor had only one boat, *Viking,* in operation. Business improved somewhat after that, however, and the *City of Milwaukee* was purchased from the Grand Trunk and put in service in November of 1978.

At present writing, *Arthur K. Atkinson* is being rebuilt and refitted, and it is expected that she will resume service in the summer of 1980. The Ann Arbor ferries are now operating under subsidy by the State of Michigan. During the winter months they run on an "as needed" basis, but a regular schedule for passenger service to Kewaunee and Manitowoc is maintained from the first of June to the middle of September.

Ann Arbor wreck, probably near Boone Hill, Herring Lake.

The Wreck on the Ann Arbor R'y.

One and one-half miles west of Sherman Sta.   Oct 20, '99.

E. B. HODGINS

PIONEER STUDY CENTER

The Empire & Southeastern Railroad

Like the Arcadia & Betsey River Railroad, the Empire & Southeastern began as a logging railroad operating on standard gauge. That it also carried passengers is almost an irrelevancy, although of course most people old enough to remember it at all, remember it as a passenger train — remember riding on it, say, from Empire to Traverse City by way of Jacktown and Empire Junction, (where one had to change cars to the Manistee & Northeastern). One proceeded via Honor, Platte River Junction (usually another change of cars), Lake Ann, Solon and Hatch's Crossing. The trip took an astonishing length of time to cover a distance of less than 25 miles as the crow flies — but, no matter, time wasn't all that important in those days.

East Empire, Maintop, Jacktown, Peterville, Stormer and the Junction were regular stops on the E&SE, but it would stop almost anywhere along the line to let people on or off. Peterville and Stormer were logging camps named after Pete Stormer, who did all the lumbering on contract for the Wilce Lumber Company. Except for a few stone foundations at Jacktown and a concrete water trough at Peterville (where the engine took on water), nothing remains of those places now.

Around 1888, the Thomas Wilce Co. of Chicago, a firm that specialized in hardwood flooring, bought a strip of land on Lake Michigan just north of the village of Empire, built a sawmill at the south end of South Bar Lake and began logging operations in the surround-

Loading Lumber, Empire, Mich.

Loading logs on the E&SE. PIONEER STUDY CENTER

Pete Stormer's log rollway at Empire Junction.
EMPIRE TOWNSHIP HERITAGE GROUP

ing timber. The Wilce company had been founded by Thomas Wilce, and in 1888 the management was taken over by his three sons, Thomas Jr., George and Harvey. Harvey Wilce came to Empire and took charge of the timber operation there, which became known as the Empire Lumber Company.

This wasn't pine country, and never had been. The rolling glacial hills around Empire were covered with virgin hardwood forest — maple, beech, oak, elm and ash, with some hemlock and basswood mixed in. The logs were huge: they had an average diameter of two and three feet for maple and beech, and up to six feet for grey elm.

Around 1890, soon after the mill was in operation, the company started to build a railroad into the Wilce timber holdings in

Empire Township and, later, in Platte Township in Benzie County. Two large docks had been built out into Lake Michigan just north of the sawmill, and now a railroad bridge was constructed across South Bar Lake opposite the South Dock. Rails were laid across the bridge and out to the end of the dock. From a "Y" at the east end of the dock (where the trains could turn around), a spur was built south to the mill. Logs brought in on the railroad were rolled off the flatcars into South Bar Lake, where they were retrieved and drawn into the mill by an endless steel chain with hooks. Sawn lumber was stacked in piles to dry near the mill, then carried to the dock on flatcars, to be loaded aboard steamers for Chicago.

Rails were also laid to the end of the north

Steam loader at Pearl Lake.
EMPIRE TOWNSHIP HERITAGE GROUP

Lumber boat *Sidney O. Neff* at Empire Lumber
Co. dock, 1912. EMPIRE TOWNSHIP HERITAGE GROUP

Largest E&SE engine and log train at Empire
Junction. EMPIRE TOWNSHIP HERITAGE GROUP

dock, which lay some 400 yards from South Dock. The north dock was used mainly for loading sailing ships with firewood slabs and edgings, and hemlock tanbark and hops for Milwaukee and Chicago.

Meanwhile, the company had ordered a locomotive from a Manistee company, and flatcars and more rails, and the mill began cutting thousands of railroad ties. According to Frank Fradd of Empire, who worked for the company as a young man, the engine was hauled across the snow from Manistee on a big horse-drawn sleigh. The flatcars and rails were shipped in by boat.

After the course had been staked out to the east, groups of workers began building the railroad grade. They used teams of horses and scrapers to level off the hillocks and fill in the low spots with sand. Flatcars followed with loads of rails and ties, and a small section of the railroad was completed each day. The road bed struck out due east for two miles, then made a long leisurely swing to the south.

In those days of railroad building, violent arguments sometimes arose over the acquisition of property rights of way. One such took place between Erastus "Rat" Dailey, the railroad construction boss, and a property owner at the south end of Empire Township, Richard Gearing.

Without even asking permission Dailey pushed the railroad grade onto Gearing's property in order to avoid a steep hill to the east. Gearing discovered the trespass and angrily ordered the construction crew off his property. Dailey offered to buy rights of way, but Gearing said nothing doing, and Dailey was forced to back up a quarter mile

Depot at Empire Junction.
EMPIRE TOWNSHIP HERITAGE GROUP

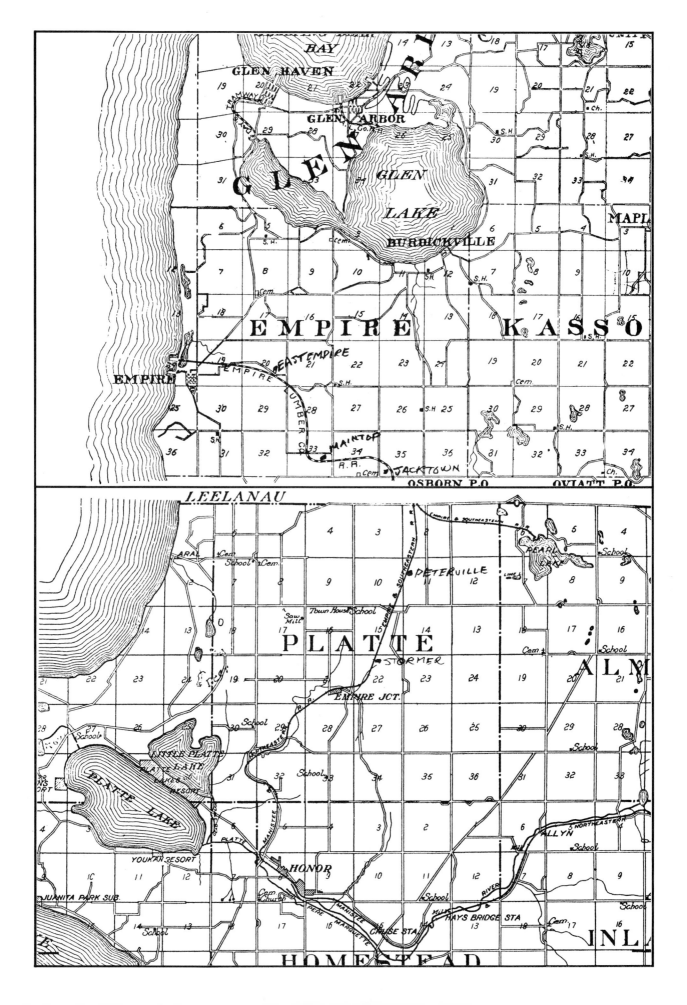

and make a cut up over the hill. (Actually, Dailey didn't back up far enough: the 1900 Leelanau County Atlas shows that the railroad cut through the northeast corner of Gearing's property.) It is said that when Harve Wilce found out about it, after returning to Empire from a trip to Chicago, he hit the roof. The short grade on Gearing's property is still visible today.

There was some consolation in the company's chagrin: a large spring was uncovered near the top of the hill, and water ran down to the tracks. A water tank was installed there, and it became a convenient place for the engine to take on water after its strenuous climb up the hill. The water stop came to be known as "Main Top", and it appears as such on county maps of that time. The railroad was first known as the Empire Lumber Co. RR, later as the Empire & Southeastern.

The first part of the railroad to be completed was the stretch from Empire to Jacktown, a distance of six miles. A few years later, a branch line of about five miles was built from Jacktown to Pearl Lake; and, around 1901, the main line was extended six miles to Empire Junction, where it connected with a branch line of the Manistee & Northeastern. Peter Stormer, boss of the logging operations, had lumber camps then at Peterville, Empire Junction and Pearl Lake.

At about that time, the company bought a larger locomotive, a passenger coach, and a caboose, and began to carry passengers on a more or less regular schedule from Empire to Empire Junction and back. A small depot was built at Empire Junction by the M&NE, and a Y which was used by both railroads. The E&SE built a larger depot at the south end of South Bar Lake. According to Fradd,

Small engine taking on water at Main Top.
EMPIRE HERITAGE GROUP

Small engine with passenger car at Empire
Depot. Oiler Jim Grant and Conductor Baker.

the first station agent was N. E. Deegan, followed by W. P. Reynolds, E. A. Voice and, finally, Harry Baker.

The train made two trips daily to Empire Junction. The first left Empire at around 7:00 in the morning and returned at noon. The second left at 2:00 p.m. and returned at 5:30. The fare from Empire to Jacktown was 20¢, and from Empire to Empire Junction, 40¢. A round trip to Empire Junction and back cost 75¢. Regular passenger calls and stops were at East Empire, Jacktown, Peterville and Empire Junction.

Most of the timber had been logged off by 1915, and in 1916 the sawmill burned down, but the passenger train continued to run until 1920. Then, in the spring of 1921, the locomotives, flatcars and caboose were sold to a Manistee company. The rails were taken up, loaded on flatcars and hauled away.

Nobody wanted the passenger coach. It sat for several years on a short section of track just north and east of Jacktown, then disappeared. Thieves working at night dismantled the car and hauled it away in trucks. They took the rails, too. Nothing was left behind except a few railroad spikes. And that was the end of the Empire & Southeastern Railroad — known affectionately in its day as the "Empire & Something Else", and the "Empire Slow and Easy".

Roundhouse and engines at Empire.

Engine No. 3 and cars at Empire dock.
EMPIRE HERITAGE GROUP

The Story of the TCL&M Railroad

The Traverse City Leelanau and Manistique Railroad came into being primarily because its parent, the Grand Rapids and Indiana Railroad, wanted a car ferry across the lake to Michigan's Upper Peninsula.

It was almost as simple as that. Ever since 1892, when the Ann Arbor Railroad opened the first cross-lake car ferry service from its slip on Betsie Lake at Elberta — first to Kewaunee, Wisconsin, then to other ports in Wisconsin and Upper Michigan — the GR&I had been envious of its railroad rival and covetous of a share in the profits from timber and mining operations in the Upper Peninsula.

Now, in 1900, in order to compete effectively with the Ann Arbor, the GR&I had to find a shorter route to the U.P., from a port somewhere between Elberta and Mackinaw City. It also had to find a northern port near the timber and the mines — a port where it would not be stifled by excessive competition. And it had to act fast, for there were others about with similar ideas.

The best bet seemed to be a ferry line between Northport and Manistique, a distance of 75 miles. The Ann Arbor was already at Manistique, having opened ferry service there in 1898. But the GR&I had a

The Afternoon Train Nearing North Port Mich 136

plan that would offset any disadvantage of being second on the scene. Of course, there was at present no railroad between Traverse City and Northport, but — no problem — the GR&I would arrange to have one built. (A direct ferry from the GR&I railhead at Traverse City was impractical because Grand Traverse Bay was usually ice-covered for two or three months of the year.)

Although the TCL&M was the GR&I's baby, the parent seems to have been reluctant to acknowledge its offspring. At the very least the GR&I wanted to keep some distance away in case the new project turned out to be a failure.

Accordingly, the task of organizing the new railroad was given to Richard R. Metheany, secretary of the GR&I and to Daniel W. Kaufman, a financier from Manistique and Chicago. Together with Charles E. Murray,

general agent at Traverse City for the GR&I, they filed articles of association for the Traverse City Leelanau and Manistique Railroad Co. with the Commissioner of Railroads on November 25, 1901. The new railroad, which was to run from Traverse City to Northport, was capitalized at $500,000. Richard Metheany was elected president and D. W. Kaufman, vice president. Murray seems to have been included in the corporation in order to give the project strong local representation and support.

Rumors about the new railroad had been abroad for several months, but the first time Traverse City people heard anything definite about it was in the late summer of 1901. Metheany and Kaufman arrived in town from Chicago on August 23, accompanied by general agent Murray. They announced their plans to a group of local businessmen,

Car ferry *Manistique No. 1* at Gill's dock, Northport. ELDEN DAME COLLECTION

including Perry Hannah, at a meeting at the Park Place Hotel.

Later, meetings were held at Northport, Suttons Bay and Bingham by agent Murray and others to drum up local support. The company hoped to raise enough local money at least to buy rights of way in Leelanau County. The amount expected from each community was $10,000 apiece from Northport and Suttons Bay townships, $5,000 from Bingham and Traverse City..Since Elmwood Township was already served by the Manistee and Northeastern Railroad, little could be expected from it.

During the next few months, most of this money was pledged by property owners in Leelanau County, particularly from those farmers, businessmen and resort owners who stood to benefit most by the railroad. The amounts pledged were roughly 3½ cents per $100 of property valuation. They were made in the form of two notes: one half payable when the railroad line was completed, one half after the railroad had been in operation for six months.

Meanwhile, a survey of the proposed route from Traverse City to Northport was made and approved. Originally, the survey called for tracks parallel to the M&NE from Traverse City to Hatch's Crossing, a distance of 5.77 miles. Before work started, however, the company decided it was more practical to contract with the M&NE for the use of its tracks over that distance. The construction contract was awarded to a Grand Rapids firm, and work on the new railroad began in the summer of 1902. Much of the grading was done by local farmers with their own teams of horses.

For a while that year, it looked to the local

people like a race between the TCL&M and the M&NE to see which would reach Northport first. In August of 1900, the Manistee & Northeastern had announced a plan to extend its Cedar City branch to Provemont (now Lake Leelanau) and on to Omena and Northport. The line to Provemont was completed in 1902, and depot grounds and rights of way to Omena were acquired. But, because of the boats operating between Leland and Fouch, there was some delay in getting permission to build a railroad bridge across the river at Provemont; and when the TCL&M started building its line, the M&NE plan was abandoned. The M&NE probably never had any intention of establishing a car ferry at Northport.

In April, 1902, a contract was made between the TCL&M and the GR&I for the operation of the new road. The GR&I was to take $75,000 worth of bonds and one-quarter of the capital stock in exchange for its services.

While all this was going on, Metheany and Kaufman were busy securing facilities at the northern end of the proposed car ferry line in the Upper Peninsula. For about $500,000 they bought the Manistique and Northwestern Railroad, a line of only 35 miles from Manistique to Shingleton. This gave them not only trackage facilities in Manistique but access there to the Minneapolis St. Paul & Sault Ste. Marie Railroad and a connection at Shingleton with the Detroit South Shore & Atlantic. The new line was named Manistique & Northern; (later it was reorganized as the Manistique & Lake Superior Railroad and extended to Doty where it made junction with the Munising Marquette & Southeastern, predecessor of the Lake Superior & Ishpeming.)

The company was capitalized at $2,000,000, with president Metheany and vice president Kaufman, and their relatives, owning most of the stock. Bonds worth $1,110,000 were also issued, with the Union Trust Co. of Detroit as trustee.

Ferry slips were built at Manistique and Northport in 1902, and a ferry was ordered from the American Ship Building Co. at Cleveland. The *Manistique Marquette & Northern No. 1*, built at a cost of $400,000, was launched in December of that year.

Soon to become known simply as the *Manistique,* she was a steel ship of 2,933 gross tons and 338 feet in length. She had a green hull, white cabins and red stacks, each with a black top and a band of blue stars on a white field. With her four tracks she could accommodate thirty railroad cars. At the time of her launching the company had plans to build a sister ship, but only the *Manistique No. 1* was ever put in service.

The Traverse City Leelanau & Manistique Railroad reached Northport in May of 1903, and on June 1 the town staged a gala celebration to welcome its coming. The first passenger train arrived at 12:45 p.m. to the blare of a brass band and cheers from the huge crowd. It bore a large group of dignitaries from Traverse City, including Julius Hannah, Senator Milliken, Frank Hamilton and many others as guests of Daniel Kaufman. They were greeted by droves of people from the town and all over the county, many of whom had brought picnic lunches.

While the band played and fifty children dressed as painted Indians whooped it up, Mrs. Kaufman drove in the last spike at the depot site. It was silver plated and garnished with red, white and blue ribbons. It bore the inscription: NORTHPORT, JUNE 1, 1903. According to a newspaper reporter, "Mrs. Kaufman drove the spike home with a vigor which excited the admiration of the crowd."

Her husband Daniel also drove in a ceremonial spike, and, after many speeches, the dignitaries repaired to Hotel Scott for more ceremony and refreshments.

Badges commemorating the event had been printed by the *Northport Leader.* On the front side was the picture of an Indian

Section crew at Suttons Bay; Park Hotel in
background was destroyed by fire in 1915.
CONRAD A. GRONSETH COLLECTION

Old Maud at Suttons Bay crossing.
CONRAD A. GRONSETH COLLECTION

medicine man, with the legend: WE ARE NOT ALL INDIANS. The reverse side bore the following inscription:

A white man's time in a red man's town. The first train at Northport on June 1, 1903. Read the Northport Leader and do not go to sleep on the tracks.

P.S. If you are contemplating suicide, jump off the dock so as not to mess up the engine with remains.

The theme of the day seems to have been that Northport was finally "out of the woods". On a big stand at the depot, decorated with red, white and blue bunting, there was a sign proclaiming that happy circumstance. Others said: "Don't Flirt with the Trainmen", "Look Out for Pick-pockets", "Those Wishing to Stop at Traverse City Must Speak to the Conductor in Advance". On a bank of gravel near the tracks was a sign, "City Bank". A clothes line between two trees was hung with suspenders, hoop skirts,

underwear and calico dresses — and a sign, "Washout on the Line". A sign at the waterfront said, "Free Drinks".

The locomotive shuttled people back and forth on free rides all afternoon from the depot to the ferry slip.

An *Evening Record* reporter wrote: "Indians by the score with wide stary eyes gazed in amazement at the locomotive as it puffed through the village, emitting great volumes of smoke. Old braves, with their squaws, sauntered about amazed at the wonders of the evidence of civilization." It seems likely, however, that the Indians were just as astonished at the antics of the whites — especially if they could read.

Service between Traverse City and Northport opened officially on June 28. The run, with stops at Bingham, Suttons Bay and Omena, took about two hours. The schedule varied somewhat over the years and with the

Celebration June 1, 1903, of first train arrival at Northport. GUYLES DAME COLLECTION

seasons, but at least one passenger train ran daily except Sunday. It left Traverse City about 3:30 p.m. and arrived in Northport at 5:30. The return trip left Northport at 8:00 p.m., reaching Traverse City around 10:00. Freight trains, of course, operated on an irregular schedule.

Ferry service between Northport and Manistique began in October, 1903. It was scheduled for three round-trip runs each week, and the passage took about eleven hours.

In November, 1903, however, the Manistique Marquette & Northern defaulted on its bonds and went bankrupt. Under the receivership of the Union Trust, control of the railroad went to the Pere Marquette. As a consequence, the car ferry, *Manistique,* was diverted to Ludington, where it entered service for the Pere Marquette with thrice weekly round-trip runs to Manistique over the next two years.

In 1905, the Pere Marquette itself went bankrupt and lost its control of the MM&N in 1906. The *Manistique* ferry then returned to her original route at Northport. Her schedule during the next two years called for departure from Northport at 10:00 a.m. on Mondays, Wednesdays and Fridays, and return from Manistique the same evenings, leaving at 9:00 p.m. The fares were $2.50 one way and $4.50 round trip. A berth cost 75¢ and meals 50¢.

On January 5, 1908, the *Manistique* had a serious accident. She struck a rock in Manistique harbor and stove in two steel plates in her hull below the engine room. Her pumps were unable to keep ahead of the leak and she sank in 17 feet of water. She was carrying a full load of cars with coal for Manistique and Minneapolis. Four days later she was raised and sent to dry dock at South Chicago.

During the next several months while she

Grand Central Depot
Omena, Mich.

NO. 20   PUBLISHED BY ORSON W. PECK, PHOTOS, TRAVERSE CITY, MICH.

Excursion

TO

MANISTIQUE

Wed=nesday JUNE 5, '07

CAR FERRY

will leave Suttons Bay dock

7:00 a. m.

Famous Juvenile Band of Suttons Bay will accompany the Excursion

Fare round trip $2.00

To Northport

Everybody come to the Queen City of the Upper Peninsula

was being repaired, the company chartered *Ann Arbor No. 1* as a replacement, and *Ann Arbor No. 2* also saw service on the Northport-Manistique run.

But freight loadings did not meet expectations, and 1908 saw the end of the Northport-Manistique car ferry service — after only five years of operation. In January the Union Trust arranged for a new company to take over the bankrupt MM&N and liquidate its assets. The *Manistique* was sold to the Grand Trunk Railroad for $237,000. Renamed *Milwaukee,* she was put in service on a regular schedule from Grand Haven to Milwaukee. Here she served until 1929, when she was lost with all hands off Milwaukee in the great storm of October 22. It was the worst single disaster to befall a Great Lakes car ferry.

The ferry slip at Northport was sold to the Ann Arbor RR, dismantled and reassembled as the west slip at Elberta.

The TCL&M continued in operation by the GR&I, but after its loss of ferry service the line soon went into a financial decline. From 1909 through 1917 it failed to show a profit. Passenger traffic increased 75% during that period (27,119 to 38,556), but freight declined proportionately even more. The GR&I gave up on it in 1914.

After that the line was operated independently until 1917, when the U.S. Government took it over for a few months during the war, to ensure movement of crops to market. In 1919 it was purchased by a local group headed by Marcus Hoyt of Suttons Bay for $65,000. Reorganized as the Leelanau Transit Company, it was leased to the Manistee & Northeastern and operated by that railroad — and its successors, the Pere Marquette and the Chesapeake & Ohio — until the present day.

During the thirties and early forties, the train with its old steam locomotive was known affectionately as old "Maud", a name given it by Will Solle, proprietor of Solle's Bookshop at Omena, who came there from Chicago in 1933. Maud was replaced by a diesel locomotive in 1946.

Passenger service was discontinued in 1948. The last freight train to Suttons Bay was in 1979; the line beyond to Northport had been abandoned in the 1960s.

The TCL&M played a big part in the lives of Leelanau County people for at least a generation. In addition to its regular stops at Bingham, Suttons Bay and Omena, you could flag the train down and get aboard almost anywhere along the line.

Leelanau farm boys of the 1920s especially remember it with affection. There were deep cuts along the 26-mile roadbed and in the winter they'd fill up so solid with drifted snow that even the big railroad plows couldn't break through. Then the farm boys would go into action with their shovels, digging out the engine from one high drift to another.

They were well paid for those days — 40¢ an hour — and sometimes if the train didn't reach its destination until after nightfall, the railroad would put them up for the night at a hotel.

"That was big money in those days," one Bingham man says. "And high living! We thought we were on top of the world!"

TCL&M plow in drift. PIONEER STUDY CENTER

Suttons Bay depot was built in 1920.
CONRAD A. GRONSETH COLLECTION

A Streetcar That Could Have Been Named 'Desire'

If Westinghouse, General Electric, or the New York capitalists had come through, Traverse City might have had a streetcar. And it might appropriately have been named "Desire"—like the one in Tennessee Williams' famous play. Certainly it was "desired" by a great number of people for a long period of time. Not only desired, but every year from 1897 to 1907 or thereabouts, a streetcar for Traverse City seemed on the very point of becoming a reality.

So much so, indeed, that Traverse City's legendary photographer Orson Peck in 1906 printed his now famous postcard showing a streetcar tooling down the middle of Front Street. The photo is of course a composite: No streetcar was ever seen in Traverse City. But the picture is less a fake than an honest anticipation of things almost certain to come. Peck believed his picture would soon come to represent reality.

It all began, back in 1893, with an editorial in the *Grand Traverse Herald*, Traverse City's first newspaper. The editor suggested that an electric railway be built between Traverse City and Old Mission, on Old Mission Peninsula. This was at a time when the use of electricity for power was just coming into popularity, and interurban electric tram lines were springing up all over the country east of the Mississippi.

The idea got a boost the following year, when prominent businessman (shoes) Frank Friedrich gave a talk on the subject at a meeting of the local businessmen's association.

Friedrich's opening remarks were, "Electricity — I'm just full of it. All you have to do is touch the button."

In a more serious vein he went on to say what a boom an electric railway would be for Traverse City. Among other things, he said, it would promote the growth of fruit farming on the Peninsula by providing fast, economical transportation for the produce; hasten the development of city suburbs; stimulate the summer resort business —much of which, he said, was being lost to places like Elk Rapids, with their convenient location on steam railroads.

Travel on an electric railway, he said, took less than half the time of cable or horse-drawn cars.

Moreover, he went on, the idea was perfectly sound from an engineering standpoint. With Traverse City's great potential for generating electricity by water power, more than adequate supply was available.

From the start it sounded like a great idea to almost everybody. And by 1897 the ball was rolling: A corporation was formed for the promotion and development of the Traverse City, Old Mission & Peninsula Railroad. Its president was Lorraine K. Gibbs, a lumber dealer in Traverse City and Kingsley, and Alderman of the Fourth Ward. Gibbs had more than a civic interest in the project: he was also an officer and stockholder in the Queen City Light and Power Co.

It was reported in the *Herald* that Gibbs had a wealthy industrialist friend in New York City who would undertake to interest eastern capitalists in the project. (This was before "capitalists" became a dirty word — except in socialist and anarchist circles.)

But first, the Corporation announced that it would seek to raise, as "good faith money," a total of $20,000 — $10,000 each from Traverse City and Old Mission Peninsula. The city money came in readily enough — Perry Hannah himself pledged $1,000 — but Peninsula Township was a little slower in coming up with the scratch. (Eventually it had to pass a bond issue, by the narrow vote of 135 to 132, to raise the money. But this was later overturned in the courts.)

Meanwhile things were humming along. In 1901 the corporation announced that rights-of-way on the Peninsula had been secured (most of it gratis) and all that was needed now (except investor money) was a franchise for the railroad from Traverse City. It estimated the total cost of the project at $200,000.

Although New York "capitalists" had not exactly stampeded to get a piece of the action, the *Evening Record,* successor to the *Herald,* happily reported that a wealthy promoter and contractor from Chicago had arrived in town with his wife to look over the ground and discuss plans and specifications with corporation officials.

The Chicago man spent all summer at the Park Place Hotel, combining business with pleasure, and, upon his departure in the fall, announced that work on the railroad probably would begin next spring. He was never heard from again. Allegedly he left the Park Place with a large unpaid bill for food and lodging.

Nothing daunted, the corporation announced next spring that both Westinghouse and General Electric were interested in the project. And in 1904 the *Evening Record* reported that Westinghouse's chief engineer was in town to survey the ground.

"When this man appears on the scene," burbled the newspaper, "things happen very quickly. His arrival indicates that work on the electric railway is about to begin."

Meanwhile, after long deliberation the city granted the railroad a charter. As originally conceived, the railroad after leaving the Peninsula would proceed down East Front Street to Union then make a loop back to Front Street by way of Union, State and Park.

But there were strong objections to laying tracks on State Street, which many people said should be reserved for the farmers with their horses and wagons. Livery stable owners B. J. Morgan and W. D. C. Germaine said they didn't mind, but the objectors prevailed and the route of the loop, if any, was left undetermined.

On Old Mission Peninsula the railroad would follow the eastern shoreline; here the roadbed was fairly level, none of the grades being more than 2 percent. Northern terminal for the railroad would be the town of Old Mission.

The Westinghouse deal unaccountably fell through, but spokesmen for the corporation continued to issue glowing progress reports. Other backers had been, or would be found; work on the project would probably begin next spring; Traverse City would have its electric railroad.

In 1903, Henry Hull, president of Oval Wood Dish Co., threw some cold water on the idea. He said it was economically unsound. He had seen the development of successful interurban lines in Ohio, he said, but the population of the Traverse City area was too sparse to support such a railroad.

He did not believe that investors could be found to back the project. As an investor himself he would not be inclined to put any money in it. Nevertheless, he would continue to lend his support in every other way.

Supporters of the railroad sniffed that Hull had every right to his opinion, but they didn't share it. The railroad, they said, was perfectly feasible both technically and economically.

And so it went, year after year. Work on the railroad was always about to begin, but nothing ever happened — not a single shovelful of earth was ever turned.

Until finally, in 1906, people who had invested in the project were growing impatient and asking for their money back. All enthusiasm gradually petered out; a year or two later the corporation was quietly dissolved and the railroad project died a natural death.

And so it was that, in spite of all the time, energy and "desire" that went into its promotion, the TCOM & PRR never got off the drawing board.

Front St. near Union,
Traverse City, Mich.

Orson Peck's composite photo, 1906.

Traverse City belles on Union Street near Front.
TRAVERSE CITY RECORD-EAGLE

Automobiles

The Abominable Automobile

The first automobile ever to appear in Traverse City was driven by a man named R. B. Cobb of Charlevoix on July 27, 1899. It created quite a stir, particularly among the horses, but the townspeople do not seem to have been all that much impressed. They called it a novelty and sport, and said it would never replace the horse.

Ten years later, however, it was obvious to almost everybody that the horseless carriage, for good or ill, was here to stay —by that time automobile manufacturers were springing up like mushrooms over the country.

PIONEER STUDY CENTER

Ford Picnic, Aug 14th 1914, Traverse City, Mich., 209 Cars. Photos by Chas J. Herbert

193

In 1906 a few affluent Traverse City people already owned the fabulous new machines. Frank Friedrich, Fred Boughey, Clarence Greilick and Ed Brosch had Cadillacs. Elsie Hannah had a Franklin and H. H. Montague, a White Steamer. Jay Blakeslee drove a Ford that was capable of doing 35 miles per hour. And Cary Hull's 1905 Royal would do 50.

In 1907 people were already complaining that cars were going too fast — "speeding up", they called it. State Street, they said, was getting to be a raceway with cars zipping along at 20 to 30 mph. Another complaint was that young children were driving automobiles on city streets. There was no law against it, no age limitations to driving an automobile. It was getting quite common to see ten- and eleven-year-olds driving cars about town, and the kids were going to kill somebody if something wasn't done about it.

The first auto accident is unrecorded, but the first fatality in Traverse City happened on the night of October 27, 1910. Two teenage couples in an Apperson "Jackrabbit" skidded on the ice at the end of Fifth Street, jumped the railroad tracks and rolled down the bank, coming to rest upside down a few feet from the river. One of the girls, Blanche Ramsey, was killed; her sister, Clara, was slightly hurt, and the two boys, Nelson Smith and Leslie Wagley, miraculously escaped injury.

In 1914, a blind Indian woman, known as

Early omnibus at Park Hotel, Suttons Bay.
CONRAD A. GRONSETH COLLECTION

Traverse City's first auto fatality, Oct. 27, 1910.
ROBERT WHITE COLLECTION

"Blind Sauba", was killed while being led down the Northport pike road near Peshaw-bestown (then known as Ahgosaville). Her name was Eliza Antoine, and she was a medicine-woman of her tribe.

That same year, Julius Campbell drove his Everett-30 on a pleasure trip of 1,874 miles to Niagara Falls and back. He went by way of Grand Rapids, Detroit and Toronto, returning via Cleveland and Toledo.

Many accidents in those days involved autos and horses. One such occurred when World's Lightweight Champion Ad Wolgast of Cadillac, on a pleasure outing with three companions, narrowly missed a horse and buggy on State Street near the Park Place Hotel. The horse reared and threw its driver, a young Traverse City woman, out of the buggy. Ad and his companions hastened to the rescue and acted like perfect gentlemen

— so the *Record-Eagle* reported — and the young lady wasn't hurt. But next day the newspaper printed a letter from an irate citizen who criticized the paper for praising the conduct of a despicable prize-fighter and suggested that Wolgast and his companions should have been run out of town.

In 1918 Charles Rennie opened the city's first gasoline service station behind his garage on the corner of State and Union. In due time it would become known as "The Pioneer Station of the North".

In that year there were already several auto dealers in town: Fisk Auto Co., 114 Park (Dodge); Charles Rennie's Oakland agency; Chevrolet Motors, 114-118 East State; Overland Motors, 311-315 East State (Overland and Willys-Knight); Grand Traverse Auto Co., West Front (organized in 1912-13 by Milton D. Bryant, brother-in-law of

Joe Vlack's delivery truck at Cedar, around 1914.

E. E. White, with Winfred White and family,
around 1915. Pratt house in background.
ROBERT WHITE COLLECTION

Harold Voice family
at Empire, 1911.
EMPIRE HERITAGE GROUP

Unidentified group at Empire.
EMPIRE HERITAGE GROUP

Henry Ford, to sell Ford cars); and one or two others.

Yet the automobile was still enough of a novelty (and a mark of distinction) in 1928 that the Polk City Directory listed the makes of automobiles after the names of Traverse City people who owned them; i.e., William Darrow (Buick), Frank Kephart (Reo), Alice Wait (Essex), Mrs. Elsie Hannah (Marmon) and so forth.

The automobile and the railroad train were bound to tangle sooner or later, and in 1919 the first recorded accident in the region happened on Sunday morning, July 6. Four young men tried to beat the GR&I *Resort Special* to a crossing at Central Lake. The iron horse won the race; two of the young men were killed, two were slightly injured, and the automobile was completely demolished.

The auto was of course no match for a train in any kind of collision. But in the end it was the automobile that would win the greater battle. It would virtually destroy all of its rivals — the railroads, the great passenger ships, city trolley cars and inter-urban lines. The last passenger line on Lake Michigan would be gone by the nineteen forties; railroad passenger service in Traverse City would end in the early fifties.

The automobile would change the face of the land, alter the life-style of all Americans, and make us the most mobile and restless people in the world since the Mongols and Genghis Khan. In 1980, on the question of whether that was good or bad — or neither — the jury of history was still out; it hadn't yet reached a verdict.

Auto owned and driven by John Lambkin.
EMPIRE HERITAGE GROUP

Early omnibus, Traverse City.
ROBERT WHITE COLLECTION

Snowmobile at Suttons Bay, 1922.
CONRAD A. GRONSETH

An Automobile Named Napoleon

In the first twenty years of the century, nearly 2,000 different makes and models of cars and trucks were turned out by some 1,000 manufacturers. Traverse City's late entry into this wide-open but ferociously competitive field was the Napoleon.

The Napoleon was named only indirectly after the general. Actually it got its name from the little town of Napoleon, Ohio, a few miles southwest of Toledo. There, in 1916, a small plant with a handful of workers began to turn out an average of one machine per day. The product found a ready acceptance in the marketplace and the company was swamped with orders, but it lacked the capital to expand production to meet the demand.

It was the brother of a local physician who was directly responsible for bringing the struggling young company to Traverse City. Elon Gauntlett, an official of the McIntyre Motor Company of Kalamazoo, had heard about the company and its problems, and early in 1917 he made a trip to Napoleon to look over the plant and talk with its people. Favorably impressed, he wrote his brother, Dr. J. W. Gauntlett, that he believed the company could be persuaded to relocate in Traverse City.

Dr. Gauntlett passed the word along to a group of prominent Traverse City businessmen, who received it with enthusiasm. They were particularly receptive to the idea because business in Traverse City at that

moment was terrible. The city was about to lose one of its two major industries, Oval Wood Dish Company, which, in July of 1917, would move to Tupper Lake, N.Y., and take with it some 200 local families, plunging the city into a severe economic decline.

Direct negotiations between the Chamber of Commerce and the Napoleon Company during the next few weeks resulted in a satisfactory deal: The Napoleon Company would move to Traverse City if a capital of $75,000 could be raised. In addition, the Chamber would grant the Company the use of the old Williams flooring factory rent-free for three years. (This building, on the river near Boardman Lake, was originally the Fulghum flooring factory; it is now the City Municipal Garage.)

A corporation known as the Traverse City Motor Car Company was formed. Its directors and officers were: W. J. Chase, President; C. E. Culver, Vice President; Frank Trude, Secretary-Treasurer; John Patchin and C. W. May. Elon Gauntlett was made General Manager and put in charge of stock sales.

The company received authorization for a capitalization of $150,000, and it was decided that the stock should be offered in $10 shares so that almost everybody in Traverse City could get a piece of the action. The town of Napoleon had already subscribed for $10,000 worth.

The stock sale campaign was launched at a public meeting at the City Opera House on

June 16, 1917, and several hundred people attended. They were informed about the company's status and proposed financing, shown pictures of the Napoleon autos and truck, and urged to get in on the ground floor by buying as much stock as they could afford. They were told that Liberty Bonds would also be acceptable as payment for stock; in fact, the company would allow a 5% premium on the Bonds. (The United States had declared war on Germany on April 6, 1917; and Traverse City people had already responded generously to the government's appeal to support the war effort.)

The company also launched a week-long advertising campaign in the *Record-Eagle*. On Monday, June 26, there was a half-page ad with the headline: "THESE PEOPLE WANT AN AUTO FACTORY AT TRAVERSE CITY — HOW ABOUT YOU?"

Under a picture of a Napoleon touring car was a list of some 300 people who had already subscribed for stock. The ad concluded with "Only Six More Days to Secure the Industry for Traverse City. EVERYBODY BOOST!"

This was followed by a big ad every day for the rest of the week, with a growing list of names. The climax came on Saturday, July 1, with a full page ad and a list of almost 1,000 names. The headline blared: "THESE PEOPLE ARE LUCKY! HOW ABOUT YOU?"

That same day the paper printed an astonishing letter:

Nearly everyone in Traverse City has been loyal to our country. We have bought Liberty Bonds and we have aided the Red Cross. Now let us be loyal to our city, Traverse City, by buying stock in the new auto company. Don't be a slacker in your home town! I am only a poor widow woman but I love Traverse City and I want to see it grow and prosper.

The letter was signed, *Mrs. J. Brown.*
Poor widow woman indeed.

On July 8, the company announced that all but $5,000 of the initial $75,000 offering had been spoken for.

Meanwhile, work on remodeling the Williams factory for its new occupants was proceeding on schedule, and by November it was ready for operation. C. A. George, manager of the Ohio plant, had come to Traverse City with his blacksmith, Martin Blaser, to oversee the final preparations.

On November 7 the public was invited to an open house at the new plant, and some 2,000 men, women and children turned out. The new plant, they found, was clean, modern and well-lighted, with plenty of lavatories and water fountains.

On display were several car and truck models. They included three types of pleasure cars — a 6-cylinder, 45 horsepower, 6-passenger touring car; a smaller, 37-horsepower, 4-passenger model; and a 37-horse, 4-passenger roadster.

A *Record-Eagle* reporter got carried away with the roadster. He described it next day as "the knobbiest little chummy sport model that has been seen in the city in many a day. It has wire wheels and a nifty one-man top. The lines are a dream and the model is a study in symmetry."

Also on display was a 32-hp, 3/4-ton truck, priced to sell at $1,085. The big touring car had a Lycoming engine; all the others were equipped with a Continental motor. The big car was priced at $1,285, the others at $1,085.

Although it was announced that car bodies and tops would be manufactured at the plant, this does not seem to have been the case until much later. The new plant assembled, painted and finished the product, but all parts and components had to be shipped in from suppliers downstate and elsewhere. This would constitute one of the company's major problems.

Some readers may be interested in the specifications of the big Napoleon touring car:
Engine: Lycoming, L-head, 45 hp.
Type: 4 cylinders en bloc
Speed: 30 mph
12-gallon gas tank

Stewart vacuum feed
Springs: semi-eliptical front, cantilever
    rear
Oiling: splashed and forced
Carburetor: Zenith
Ignition: Connecticut
Cooling system: thermo-syphon
Starting and lighting: Dyneto
Lamps: double-bulb nitrogen
Transmission: single unit with motor,
    3-speed
Brakes: equalizing on 12½" drums
Rear axle: semi-floating
Stewart speedometer, ammeter, sight
    oil-gauge, clock, electric horn
    under hood
Wheelbase: 112 inches
Weight: 2300 lbs.

At the open-house meeting on November 7 there were speeches by some of the company directors and others. John Patchin said enthusiastically, "There is every evidence that our company will be a hummer. It is your patriotic duty to become a member of this company, for it is going to be the savior of our city."

And L. L. Tyler, Superintendent of Traverse City schools, weighed in with, "We are presented with an opportunity to climb out of the old rut of industrial stagnancy. We are going to put Traverse City on the map, and we are going to have a city of 20,000 inhabitants by 1920 if not before. I am going to double my original subscription tonight, even if I have to pay for it on the installment plan."

Afterward, salesmen moved about through the crowd, selling stock. Then the floor was cleared and the guests danced until midnight to the music of Clifford Mull and his six-piece orchestra.

Despite this cheerful beginning, the plant was slow getting into operation, and in December Elon Gauntlett was replaced as general manager by E. D. Misner of Kalamazoo. Misner was touted as a man of wide experience in the auto field. And it was considered significant that he had so much faith in the Napoleon that he was willing to take the job on a commission basis.

"We have orders for half a million cars," he announced. "Soon we'll be turning out three a day. We are going to pay a dividend of 6% this year, and I am going to make a lot of money too. If I wasn't sure of that, I wouldn't be here."

Fine and dandy — with a man like that at the helm how could the company fail to be a winner? But it soon became apparent that enthusiasm alone wasn't enough. Lack of operating capital continued to plague the fledgling company.

In March of 1918 it faced a crisis.

The City of Cadillac had made a bold bid for the plant, and a few disgruntled stockholders were in favor of the move. Misner himself, sore at not having received any commission money, was reported to be dealing with Cadillac officials. He was said to have told them that the company would be successful if it were not in Traverse City. An offer came from the Cadillac group to buy all outstanding Napoleon stock at a full 100 cents on the dollar. Stockholders were urged to support the move to Cadillac.

Stung by this impudence, the Chamber of Commerce called an immediate council of war. Secretary W. J. Hobbs opened it with, "Gentlemen, if we are not going to get behind this project and stay behind it, we had better dump it right now." He added that the loss of the factory would deal Traverse City a psychological blow from which it might never recover.

Speaker after speaker called for an all-out effort to sustain the company. Whatever Cadillac could do, they said, Traverse City could do better. The upshot was a strong resolution pledging the Chamber and the city to back the company with all its resources.

Since the pressing need was for cash to meet the company's $300 weekly payroll, another stock sale campaign was launched to sell the remaining $45,000 of the original $150,000 capitalization. Teams of the "city's 20 liveliest businessmen" cruised up and down the city streets urging people to buy Napoleon stock and save the city from economic ruin. New Napoleon automobiles were parked in line on Front Street so that everybody could see and examine them.

The campaign was only moderately successful. Some $20,000 of stock was sold—enough to keep the wheels turning for a while. Meanwhile, production at the factory was limping along at something less than one car a day.

In June a new manager was hired to replace E. D. Misner, who had been let go at the time of the Cadillac affair. He was J. W. Oswald, a machinist and toolmaker who had organized the Oswald Motor Company of Goshen, Ind., in 1911. He was described by the *Record*

Eagle as "a chubby fellow of middle age with a kindly disposition and an uncanny knowledge of mechanics".

At a board meeting in August, 1918, the directors voted to increase capitalization from $150,000 to $500,000. They also decided to change the company name from Traverse City Motor Car to Napoleon Motors. Oswald reported that an order for 430 cars and trucks had just been received from a dealer in Dallas.

In December, the company announced that its 1918 production totaled 95 passenger cars and 25 trucks. Better progress, however, was in store for 1919.

In the spring of that year four downstate men offered to invest $20,000 in the company and to take over the reins of management. They were W. C. Rath, C. D. Peet, Stanley Rae and W. H. Schmaltz. All were now working — or had recently worked — for the

This may be Traverse City's first recreational vehicle, built for Stanley Rae, sales manager at Napoleon Motors. Rae second from left, Henry C. Carter seventh from left; seated fourth from left is Nels Oleson, father of Gerald Oleson.

PIONEER STUDY CENTER

Republic Truck Company of Alma, Mich.

A check of their credentials at Republic elicited nothing but glowing recommendations, and the new team was signed aboard in May. Peet and Rath, who were made business manager and general manager respectively, moved to Traverse City and established their families in houses on prestigious Sixth Street.

Interviewed by a *Record-Eagle* reporter, Rath declared confidently, "Just give us a few weeks and we will show you a decided change in the local plant. Watch our smoke!"

The stockholders had heard that one before, but this time it proved to be no idle boast. Within a short time the new management had streamlined production, ironed out some of the kinks in the supply line, set up an efficient bookkeeping system and developed a nationwide sales organization. Soon the plant was turning out three machines per day, and orders were pouring in from all over the country.

Things kept on at this heady pace throughout the year — it looked as if the company was off and running at last. By November 50 men were working 10 hours a day at the plant, and production was up to five cars a day. That same month the company increased its production facilities by doubling the size of the factory basement (it had been a half basement), and putting up a new building on the site of the Campbell Folding Crate Co., which had burned down in October. Due to the slow start, total production for 1919 was 125 cars and 125 trucks.

Production was still lagging far behind new orders. For this reason — and because it was selling many more trucks now than passenger cars — the company decided to eliminate cars and concentrate its production entirely on trucks. It now began to produce several different sizes and models of trucks, all of which could be customized to suit the buyers' needs. The plant was now manufacturing its own bodies, seats and cabs, and

was buying its frames from the Traverse City Iron Works.

1920, at least the first half of it, was a banner year for Napoleon. Production rose to more than five trucks per day, and shipments were made to such far-away places as Calcutta, Antwerp and London. During a railroad strike, a six-wheeled Napoleon truck went to New York under its own power, carrying a regular one-ton truck for shipment to the Orient. In keeping with its new prosperity company officials moved into a suite of offices in the Traverse City State Bank building.

In February the company declared a 5% dividend. But the certificate was good only for the purchase of more stock. Some of the stockholders were miffed because the stock was now selling for $15 instead of the original $10. But Julius Steinberg, owner of Steinberg's clothing store and builder of Steinberg's Opera House, reassured them. "Don't give away your Napoleon stock certificates just because you have to pay $15 a share," he announced in a *Record-Eagle* half-page ad. "If you don't care to use them, we will buy them at full value."

At a banquet for company employees in March, general manager Rath announced that every Napoleon worker with a year of service or less would receive a paid-up $1,000 life insurance policy. This would be increased each year by $100 up to a maximum of $1,500.

And in May the company offered to provide vegetable-garden plots to all its workers, who now numbered 85. The company would plow, drag and fertilize a 3½-acre strip of land adjacent to the plant on Boardman Lake and the River.

But supply problems continued to plague the company. The Great War had brought about an acute shortage of steel, and the railroads, given a temporary new lease on life by the war effort, were now in a rapid and irreversible decline. In a speech to the Lions

Club Rath complained bitterly, "The railroad and the power situation is rotten."

In July the company increased its capitalization to $2,500,000 and launched another stock sale campaign. The company wasn't financially embarrassed, company officials explained, far from it. The money was needed for future expansion. There were $4,000,000 worth of orders on the books, and business was never better.

Then the roof fell in. By October the country was in the grip of a severe economic depression. Business and industry all over the world ground to a halt.

From this point on, everything at Napoleon Motors went downhill fast. By February 1921 the work force was down to 13 men, and production was almost nil. Sales were non-existent; no orders were coming in. Rath issued a cheerful statement that the company was in excellent condition, weathering the economic storm in fine shape. But he was whistling in the dark — no one knew how long the recession might last.

In February also, to almost everybody's surprise, the company issued a 10% stock dividend. It was in the form of scrip, with 8% as additional stock and 2% redeemable for cash in August. This was virtually the company's last gasp — although it lingered on for another two years. During that time, except for occasional small spurts, the plant was mostly idle.

In 1923 a move was made to revive the company under new management, but the effort died aborning. Early that year the company was forced into bankruptcy by its creditors. The creditors numbered 100; liabilities were $110,000; assets almost none.

In the fall of 1923 the plant was sold to the Zapf Fruit Package Company, a manufacturer of baskets. When Zapf went out of business in 1926, the City bought it for $15,000 for use as a municipal garage.

In retrospect it seems clear — quite aside from the question of its desirability — that an automobile factory for Traverse City just wasn't a very good idea. Even if it had somehow been able to get through the recession of 1921-1922, it probably could not have survived the Great Depression of the Thirties. It was too far from its sources of materials and supplies, too far from its major markets, too dependent upon a failing supply line.

During the six years of its existence, the company sold $650,000 worth of stock to some 3,000 investors, and in the end, of course, it was all worthless. If it now seems somewhat reprehensible on the part of the Chamber of Commerce and the city's prominent businessmen to promote the sale of stock in a private company on the basis of patriotism, in all fairness it should be pointed out that most of them probably really believed that the company would lift the city out of its economic doldrums. One is inclined, at least, to give them the benefit of the doubt.

One final note: Steinberg Brothers' offer to redeem stock certificates at full value ($10 worth of merchandise for each $10 certificate) met with an enthusiastic response. In fact, the firm redeemed so much stock that it soon followed Napoleon Motors into bankruptcy.

Airplanes

And, In The Air...

Transportation in the Grand Traverse region entered the third dimension on October 17, 1909, when Charles Augustine, a daring and inventive young Traverse City man, flew his own airplane off Rennie Hill south of town.

The plane was of Augustine's own make — a biplane (the Record-Eagle reporter called it a "double-decker") 20 feet long by four feet wide. The plane had no engine, and so Charlie had four of his friends run with the craft — two at each wing — until it got airborne. The plane dipped down below the brow of the hill, and the crowd thought Charlie was a goner for sure; but then it came swooping up, pretty as a waterbird, and glided to a soft landing 600 feet away. The crowd cheered, photographers took snapshots and Charlie did it all over again to prove it was no fluke. It was the first time Traverse City had ever seen an airplane.

Next day, the paper printed the story and swore it was all true and even invited doubters to come down and look at the photographs, which were too dark to print but nevertheless clear enough to satisfy anyone. The paper reported that Augustine was elated by the flight, because, he said, most airplanes of this design fell out of the sky like a rock when the engine quit, whereas his plane, without an engine, made a beautiful landing. He announced that a new airplane of his design and with a six-cylinder engine was being built for him by W. A. Campbell, chief engineer at the basket factory. Unfortunately, the records do not show what became of this airplane or of Charlie Augustine himself.

But Traverse City had clearly entered the space age, and one thing followed another. In November of 1911, a barnstorming pilot put on a two-day exhibition and flew his plane off 12th Street and around the Asylum grounds at 200 feet in the air. On one of his landings, however, his rear landing wheel hit a stump and badly punctured its tire, which put him out of commission for that day.

In April of 1926 a group of 50 Traverse City businessmen bought a 60-acre tract on top of Ransom Hill south of Rennie Street for $6,000 and offered to maintain it as a landing field for two years. After that time, they said, they hoped to sell it, at no profit, to the City or to a private air-minded group. The field had been in use for around five years and it was officially registered by the National Aeronautic Association.

Their plans were shot down, however, two years later when a bond issue of $8,000, enabling the City to buy the tract, was defeated by three votes. The Ransom site meanwhile had been declared unsuitable by an airport engineer and consultant, and an airport commission was appointed by mayor James T. Milliken to come up with an alternative plan for a city airport.

The Ransom airport was still in use in 1930, when a Grand Rapids group established the Jack Byrne's air service from that city to Harbor Springs. The Furniture Capital Air Service (also known as the Michigan Air Express) had connections with the Kohler Aviation Corporation of Wisconsin and had already established an air schedule from Grand Rapids to Milwaukee and other Wisconsin points.

The schedule to Traverse City began in

Orson Peck's fanciful composite photo of
Charles Augustine's flight. ROBERT WHITE COLLECTION

Chas. Augustine, Traverse City's Aviator
making a flight over the City

July of 1930, and the first flight was in command of the company's chief pilot, Floyd Beeker. The plane left Traverse City at 2:46 in the afternoon and arrived at Grand Rapids at 4:37; northbound, the flight left Grand Rapids at 10:30 and arrived at Traverse City at 12:21 in the afternoon. There were 10-minute stops at Big Rapids, Cadillac, Traverse City and Charlevoix, and 23 minutes at Petoskey. Later, the schedule was changed to permit Traverse City people to leave town early in the morning and return from Grand Rapids in the afternoon.

Two years later, Traverse City witnessed a thrilling exhibition of daredevil flying when Barney Goloski, a parachute jumper from Detroit, stole a plane at Ransom Field and spent a hair-raising 15 minutes diving under telephone wires and hopping over buildings. He finally crashed two miles south of town but walked away from the wreck with only a small cut over his left eye.

Goloski explained in Parm Gilbert's court next day that he had purchased liquor from a stranger near Silver Lake (this was during Prohibition, of course) and had got drunk; otherwise he would never have done what he did, as he had only slight flying experience. The judge marveled at his apparent proficiency but gave him 4-5 years at Ionia.

A new airport for Traverse City finally got under way in February, 1935, when a crew of 38 men on a WPA project began clearing 360 acres of city-owned property east of Garfield Avenue (the present airport site). The work was completed in 1936 at a cost of $50,000, and the Ransom field was officially closed. In the following year, a "huge" 28-passenger Boeing deluxe airliner, sponsored by the Rennie Oil Company, landed at the airport in May with a plane-load of state and city dignitaries. The plane had a top speed of 150 mph and carried a crew of six.

Penn Central Airlines opened a regularly

Ransom Airport in the middle 1920s.

scheduled air passenger service in July, 1938, and a huge crowd was on hand to greet the first arrival. The northbound flight from Detroit to the Soo reached Traverse City at 9:14 a.m., and again at 4:33 in the afternoon. The airline's equipment consisted of two Boeing 247-Ds, carrying 10 passengers plus the pilot and copilot; top speed was 200 mph. Another milestone was passed on July 20 when Penn Central carried the first air mail from Traverse City. Postmaster Jerome Wilhelm announced that over 3,000 Traverse City letters went out. In June of that year, Rennie Oil Co. received its first shipment of aviation gasoline.

A major improvement and enlargement of the Traverse City airport was completed in 1940 at a cost of $150,000; this also was a WPA project.

In 1946 the Federal Trade Commission ruled that a railroad could not operate an airline, and a new company, Capitol Airlines, was formed to take over from Penn Central, which was owned and operated by the Penn Central Railroad. The new company, with a fleet of Douglas DC-3s, (and later, DC-4s) continued to expand air service to Traverse City; by 1953, for example, the City had 10 flights a day during the summer.

In 1960 Capitol Airlines was bought by United Airlines, which suspended service to Traverse City and other Michigan points. This caused great concern to Traverse City officials and business people, but in January of 1961 it was announced that flight service in Michigan had been awarded to a Wisconsin airline, North Central. This company took over Capitol's schedule and continued to improve air service, operating with the Convair prop-jets 440 and 580 and, beginning in July of 1971, with Douglas DC-9 jet aircraft.

It was to accommodate this jet-plane service and for other reasons that a $3

million improvement to the Traverse City airport was made in 1970. The old terminal building, built by the Navy as an operation building in 1943, was replaced by an impressive new airport facility, including a separate building for general aviation. The east-west runway was lengthened to 6,500 feet, and a new north-south runway completed.

In 1979 North Central Airlines was merged with Southern Airlines and the new company, Republic Airlines, became a major carrier with air service from continental coast to coast. In the summer of 1980, Traverse City had a total of 16 incoming and outgoing flights each day, and the equipment consisted almost entirely of DC-9 jet aircraft, the Convair 580s being nearly phased out.

The rapid growth of air travel in the Grand Traverse region is illustrated by the following figures. Passenger volume increased from 4,818 in 1948 to 27,245 in 1967, and to 172,455 in 1979.

Republic DC-9. Shown on steps is Captain Philip M. Wakefield, son of the authors, who was born and raised in Traverse City.

Bibliography

BOOKS

Barnes, Al, *Vinegar Pie and Other Tales of the Grand Traverse Region.* Detroit, 1959.

Barry, James, *Ships of the Great Lakes.* Berkeley, 1973.

Berman, Bruce D., *Encyclopedia of American Shipwrecks.* Boston, 1972.

Bowen, Dana Thomas, *Shipwrecks of the Lakes.* Cleveland, 1969.

Dunbar, Willis F., *All Aboard! A History of Railroads in Michigan.* Grand Rapids, 1969.

Elliott, Frank, *When Railroad was King.* Lansing, 1965, 1966.

Fitting, James E., *The Archeology of Michigan.* New York, 1970.

Frederickson, Arthur C. and Lucy, *Early History of the Ann Arbor Carferries.* Frankfort, Mich., 1949.

_____, *Later History of the Ann Arbor Carferries, Boats 6 & 7.* Frankfort, 1951.

Fuller, George M., *Historic Michigan, Land of the Great Lakes.* 3 vols., Dayton, 1924.

Hatcher, Harlan and Erich A. Walter, *The Great Lakes, a Pictorial History.* New York, 1963.

Havighurst, Walter, *The Long Ships Passing.* New York, 1975.

Hilton, George, *The Great Lakes Car Ferries.* Berkeley, 1962.

Ivey, Paul Wesley, *The Pere Marquette Railroad Company.* Lansing, 1919.

Koch, Michael, *The Shay Locomotive, Titan of the Timber.* Denver, 1971.

Leach, Dr. M. L., *A History of the Grand Traverse Region.* Traverse City, 1883.

Littell, Edmund M., *100 Years in Leelanau.* Leland, 1965.

May, George S., *Pictorial History of Michigan.* 2 vols., Grand Rapids, 1967.

Moore, Charles, *History of Michigan.* Chicago, 1915.

Powers, Perry E., *A History of Northern Michigan.* 3 vols., Chicago, 1912.

Quimby, George Irving, *Indian Life in the Upper Great Lakes, 11,000 B.C. to A.D. 1800.* Chicago, 1960.

Ratigan, William, *Great Lakes Shipwrecks and Survivals.* New York, 1960.

Schoolcraft, Henry R., *Journal of Travels.* Mentor William Edition, East Lansing, 1953.

Sprague, Elvin L. and Mrs. George N. Smith, *History of Grand Traverse and Leelanaw Counties.* Indianapolis, 1903.

Stonehouse, Frederick, *Isle Royale Shipwrecks.* Au Train, Mich., 1977.

Stroup, Donald, *The Life and Death of Railroad, The Manistee and Northeastern.* Michigan Historical Commission, Lansing, 1964.

The Traverse Region, H. R. Page & Company. Chicago, 1884.

Vent, Myron H., *South Manitou Island.* Springfield, Va., 1973.

Wait, S. E. and W. S. Anderson, *Old Settlers of the Grand Traverse Region.* Traverse City, 1918.

ARTICLES AND PAPERS

Brinkman, James H., *The Fleet that Vanished: The Growth and Decline of the Passenger Trade in Northwestern Lower Michigan.* Student paper, Western Michigan University, 1966.

Burton, Robert E., *Car Ferry to Northport: Broken Link to the Upper Peninsula.* Michigan History, Vol. 51, pp. 1-17, 1967.

Cowles, Walter C., *Steam Navigation on the Inland Lakes of Antrim County.* Series of articles in the *Antrim County News,* August 25 to October 12, 1960.

Dancey, Thomas B., *Chicago to Mackinac, Story of the Northern Michigan Transportation Company.* Michigan History, Vol. 30, pp. 457-465.

Edson, Marjorie, *The History of the Arcadia and Betsey River Railroad.* Student term paper, Central Michigan University, n.d.

Johnson, David L., *Around Carrying Point, A Short History of Nineteenth Century Harbor Development in Northport, Michigan.* Student paper, Northwestern Michigan College, Traverse City, 1970.

Lamphere, Helen F., *The Grand Rapids and Indiana Railroad.* Student term paper, Central Michigan University, 1968.

Thayer, George W., *From Vermont to Lake Superior in 1845.* Michigan Pioneer and Historical Collections, Vol. 30, pp. 549-566.

Walton, Ivan H., *Great Lakes History, 1615-1815.* Michigan History, Vol. 25, pp. 276-299.

_____, *Developments on the Great Lakes, 1815-1943.* Michigan History, Vol. 27, pp. 72-142.

Webb, Charles J., *Hannah, Lay and Company, A Study in Michigan's Lumber Industry.* Master thesis, Wayne State University, Detroit, 1938.

NEWSPAPERS

These newspapers (on microfilm at the Mark Osterlin Library, Northwestern Michigan College at Traverse City, Mich.), were a prime source of material: *Antrim County News, Benzie Banner, Benzie County Patriot, Elk Rapids Progress, Grand Traverse Herald, Kalkaska Kalkaskian, Leelanau County Times, Leelanau Enterprise, Northport Leader, Suttons Bay Courier, Traverse Bay Eagle, Traverse City Morning Record, Traverse City Evening Record* and *Traverse City Record-Eagle.*

ATLASES

Antrim County, 1897, Philadelphia.

Benzie County, 1901, Knoxville, Tenn.

_____, 1915, Chicago

Grand Traverse County, 1881, Philadelphia.

_____, 1895, Philadelphia.

_____, 1908, Chicago.

Leelanau County, 1900, Knoxville, Tenn.

Index